The Housewife Loved a Bandit

(Hey Ma, what were you thinking?)

by

Larry Baran

For Nancy and Freddie

Hyde Park Historical Society

Presents:

Hyde Park's Bonnie & Clyde

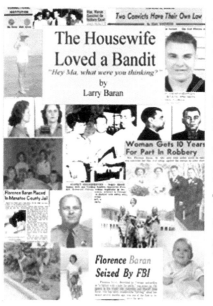

Larry Baran, author of *The Housewife Loved a Bandit*, will show and tell how his mother, Flo Baran, escaped Hyde Park into a life of crime, what happened on the crime spree, and how it all came to an end.

The story starts at 5400 S. Ridgewood in 1954.

Copies of the book will be available for $10.

Saturday, March 7, 2020
2:00 - 4:00 pm
Hyde Park Historical Society
5529 S. Lake Park Avenue

For more information, contact HPHS at 773-493-1893; info@hydeparkhistory.org.
www.hydeparkhistory.org

Published by Larry Baran.
All rights reserved

ISBN 13: 978-0-9992719-0-2
ISBN 10: 09992719-0-3

Printed in the United States of America

Copyright 2017
1st edition
English language version

For more information and newspaper articles from the 1950's visit the
website   www.mightymoonmen.com   and sign the guestbook.

Credit where credit is due

The author gives many thanks to all of the people, places and things who assisted in the development of this long overdue story. First of all, my lovely spouse who casually suggested one day that I might be able to find some info about my mother's past on the internet. That search was the spark that got this fire going. Also, relatives, friends, enemies, acquaintances, critics, government agencies, law enforcement, websites, people who confuse armadillos with aardvarks and anteaters, other authors and media outlets all contributed priceless morsels of information without whom I never would have had a clue about who, what, where, how, when, and why all this happened.

Special thanks go out to Billy Cox and the staff of the Sarasota Herald Tribune. Billy interviewed me, my sister Jeanne and other individuals to put together a front page article about my mother. The story entitled "THE MYSTERIES OF MA FLO" was published on Mother's Day, May 8, 2011. It's an expertly crafted piece about my search for my mother's past and the several "missing years" in the 1950's when she was a guest of the Florida Department of Corrections. That report gave me the inspiration to doggedly continue pretending to be an investigative journalist for the writing of this book. The article has been safely tucked away in digital form for all of us to savor in the Sarasota Herald Tribune website archives.

Of course, I need to thank my mother Florence and her free-wheeling adventurous spirit. The accounts of her unabashed conduct back then became a gift to me in my later years. What else do I have to do in my retirement but write a book?

That being said, every effort has been made to confirm the accuracy of the documents, pictures, rumors and innuendos included in this writing. Alas, not every picture I used could be "fixed" to perfection but they all help tell the story as is. To my knowledge, no "alternative facts" have been included. I must offer my sincere apologies if I screwed up any of this.

The Housewife Loved a Bandit - Chapters

Song

I got the walkaway walkaway blues
The kind of walkaway blues I can't lose
I'm gonna leave this town
ain't gonna hang around
I got the walkaway walkaway blues

I got the walkaway walkaway blues
I'm gonna get me some walkaway shoes
I'm gonna see new sights
and other city lights
I got the walkaway walkaway blues

Now I'm all through with dreamin'
It's time for me to start anew
and all my fancy schemin'
isn't likely to come true
and that's why

I got the walkaway blues
right down to my walkaway shoes
I'm gonna pack my sack
and I ain't lookin' back
I got the walkaway walkaway blues
oh yeah!
I got the walkaway walkaway blues.

- Florence Baran

"……..a fighter with a taste for raw garlic"

FBI. US Marshals. Uniformed Chicago Police. Ma went down swinging that day against men with badges, warrants and handcuffs. It was a violent encounter. They needed five men to force her, still scratching, punching, kicking and screaming, into the back seat of the unmarked car.

Other than that, July 26th, 1954, was a peaceful picture-perfect sun-drenched summer day in Chicago's Hyde Park neighborhood. The 57th Street beach was teeming with children and their families enjoying the emerald waters of Lake Michigan. The whole city was excited about the arrival of the captured U505 German submarine. It was soon to become a permanent exhibit at the Museum of Science and Industry. I was 4 years old.

My grip was just about exhausted when my sister Nancy
finally snapped the shutter on her good old Brownie camera.
Author's Collection

The air was warm-weather fresh with the thick humid perfume of our trees, flowers and lovely lilac bush. The triple-trunk sumac tree in the front yard was a marvel to me. I could not resist climbing it and my sister Nancy could not resist taking my picture while I hugged my favorite tree trunk.

Our house had recently been treated to a new layer of white stucco. The window and porch trim had a fresh coat of dark green oil based paint. My dad was very proud of his castle, the first home he had ever bought. He systematically made one improvement after another since purchasing that two-story corner house at 5400 S. Ridgewood Court in December, 1950. For him, the house was a constant and a source of great pride. He would do whatever was necessary to improve that 1890's structure anytime he wanted. He was in control. His wife, however, was another story.

My oldest sister Nancy on guard duty with our ever-present Collie dog.
Enter at your own risk – nice dog, dangerous sister!
Author's Collection

So, what exactly happened on that fine summer day? That summer day began last year. Ma abruptly left the family soon after Halloween of 1953. She apparently needed a break from the momma/housewife routine and took full advantage of her time-out. The Housewife came back home from her "vacation" seven months later just in time for my fourth birthday.

Around June 10th, 1954, with a fully refreshed soul and a fully refilled gas tank, she hopped into her 1951 black-over-cream Chevy and sped back to her sweet home in Chicago. My mother's journey north began in Miami, Florida. Ma stopped along the way and bought a dozen watermelons. She didn't want to arrive home empty-handed after such a prolonged absence. That juicy sticky summer fruit is always a treat. I suspect she didn't want to miss my birthday on June 22nd and my sister Loretta's on July 22nd. Lot's of special days to share once again. But....hmmm... why was she in Florida?

We had a gloss-white wringer washing machine in the basement. To this four-year-old, it was a beast – big, noisy and scary. Once I came within milliseconds of those rubber-coated wringer rollers gobbling up my left hand. A narrow escape and a lesson learned! With six kids and two adults in the house, the machine was in constant use. On this summer day, old monster-lips decided to malfunction. The local "Woodlawn and 53rd Street Laundromat" was necessary and convenient.

Ma came out to our shady front yard to get her little helper. Since I was the youngest of six, she often included me on her errands around the neighborhood so the others would not have to be bothered watching their whiney pot-bellied, crybaby snot-nosed little brother. I was always excited about going for a ride. It was my chance to get away from those domineering bratty big sisters and their giggling friends always teasing me about one thing or another. Actually, they were usually very nice to me but there were those "moments" where kids will be kids, practicing the fine art of dominance and submission,.

I'd ride shotgun-in-the-Chevy and could recite the make of cars we passed. Ma thought I was smart like that but, who knows, I could have been wrong. Your author was probably just throwing out car names heard before and Ma didn't know any better. I learned at an early age the value of a well-worn axiom, "*If ya can't dazzle 'em with brilliance, ya baffle 'em with BS.*" That technique came in handy during my technical teaching career many years hence.

I followed her down the creaky wooden steps into the shadows of the musty basement to help pack pillowcases with dirty towels, clothes and bed sheets. The late afternoon sunlight streaming through a west-facing window provided light for our task. We trudged back up the basement stairs and out through the front door allowing the screen door to slam shut. After the bags bounced down the newly painted front porch steps, we dragged them over the sidewalk towards the front gate. I waved to our family friend, Leroy "Skeeter" Boarman who had come by to play with me and my older brother Freddie.

Ma's '51 Chevy was parked facing east on 54th Street just a few feet west of Ridgewood Court. We set the bulging pillowcases down in the street behind the car and Ma opened the trunk. She busily arranged the laundry bags as I looked on from the sidewalk by the white picket fence. The sun was at my back so I figure it was about 4 o'clock in the afternoon.

Suddenly, a dozen black cars zoomed up and screeched to a halt. We lived on a corner so they came from four different directions. In an instant, there were police everywhere as if they appeared out of the thin air. Three large men in suits ran up and grabbed ma. The word "chaos" pretty much describes the scene.

Loretta and your author share some face time with Spitfire the black cat and our other kitty, good ol' "what's-its-name". On July 26, 1954, Ma's '51 Chevy was just about where that car is parked. Damn, I was cute!
Author's Collection

My mother's primal instincts kicked into high gear and she was fighting like a wild beast. I'm sure she screamed something that sounded like *"Get your fluxing hands off me!"* This high-decibel response was a classic demonstration of Ma's spontaneous nature. The best defense is a great offense. On that day, Flo Baran was exceptionally defensively offensive.

Who the hell were these guys? Unbeknownst to the kindly Mrs. Baran, she was wrestling US Marshals executing a fugitive arrest warrant. Within one thin moment, it became abundantly clear that the three US Marshals needed more than three US Marshals to execute *this* fugitive arrest warrant. By all accounts, she was kicking ass. Two uniformed Chicago Police officers jumped in. Finally cuffed and still kicking, our 36-year-old mother disappeared into the back seat of the waiting prowl car.

In the middle of all this, my brother Fred appeared clutching his prized baseball bat. At 9 years old, he had the blind courage and loyalty to attack those big guys who were dragging away his mother. He didn't see men in uniforms with badges, guns and clubs. As far as he knew, strangers were stealing his mom. Before Freddie could launch someone's noggin over the left field fence, an officer wrapped up my brother and pulled him away.

Skeeter Boarman was still there, a stunned witness to the commotion. He asked a neighbor who was standing by, *"Why are they arresting Mrs. Baran?"* Someone overheard a cop say something about armed robberies.

According to the FBI and newspaper accounts, it was a violent encounter. It took five men to corral dear old Ma and slip on the bracelets.

The FBI described her as:

> *-a woman who liked to fight*

and

> *-a fighter with a taste for raw garlic*

It is a rare occasion when someone's mama is the subject of a dramatic arrest. All this begs the question; "What did she do to get this kind of attention?" Didn't she have a nice home with a white picket fence? Didn't she share this home with a hard-working husband and father? Wasn't this the idyllic 1950's baby boomer days when black-and-white TVs reflected and/or encouraged happy post-war family stability with every daily crisis resolved just in time for dinner right-after-a-word-from-our-sponsors?

What in tarnation just happened here? US Marshals? Chicago Police? Handcuffs and four-letter words? Why did those dirty coppers, in broad daylight, steal away the mother of a confused and sobbing little boy left clutching that white picket fence? Could all of this police pandemonium been a tragic case of mistaken identity? Was there a back-story here lurking behind the "Leave-It-To-Beaver" image of domestic normalcy? Did something naughty happen during my ma's seven-month vacation? Yeah, probably. Otherwise, I would have no story to tell and would just be wasting your time with this dead end chapter one. So, let's get down to business. At this point, it is incumbent upon me to paraphrase the words of the immortal Ricky Ricardo, *"You got some 'splainin' to do, Florence."*

14 year-old Nancy towers over her younger sisters and the family collie in this summer 1953 photo taken just before their mother "packed her sack and didn't look back."
Author's Collection

How did a mother of six and a party-animal parolee become an item? They didn't wake up one morning, meet at a Hyde Park tavern for peanuts and beer and then make a life-changing spontaneous decision to criss-cross the country raising hell. Or did they? It was exciting for me to investigate where they came from, how they were raised and who influenced them during their formative years. Ya know, we gotta blame somebody.

My Mother, The Housewife, Florence Mary Wilczynski (Wills)

Long before she was a wanted fugitive, Florence was just a little girl growing up in the Chicago area. Mom (DOB March 30, 1918) was the middle sister to Stella the oldest (March 7, 1916), and Helen (January 15, 1920). The girls, all Chicago born, received their Polish names at birth: Stefany, Florencja and Helena.

The girls were born to my grandparents, Polish immigrants John Wilczynski and Agata Kwarciak. Both were from small towns in Southern Poland. John was born June 25, 1892, in Przyszowa, while Agata was born February 5, 1898, in Kobylec.

John and Agata arrived in New York in 1913 and 1911 respectively, part of the early 20th century migration of peoples from Eastern Europe. They both sailed across the big pond in the steerage quarters of the SS St. Paul. That ship made regular voyages ferrying passengers between New York and England.

An interesting historical note: the SS St Paul was used in Guglielmo Marconi's first ship-to-shore radio communication in 1899.

John arrived here one year after the legendary allegedly unsinkable Titanic lost an argument with an uncompromising iceberg. Titanic's ill-fated maiden voyage fostered nightmarish imaginings in the minds of hopeful travelers. While savoring a refreshing *zimne piwo* in hometown Przyszowa, I can imagine young John expressing doubt about traveling by saying to his best friend Stanley *"Teraz skoro Titanic jest na dnie morza, czy jest jakas inna sposob jak mozemy dostac sie do Chicago?"* or something like that. Since the "friendly skies" were not yet available, my maternal Grampa had to settle for transportation in the proletariat level of a ship on the high seas.

The couple met and soon married in Chicago, September 14, 1914. They wed at St. Ann's Parish Church at 18th and Leavitt streets. According to the 1920 census, the Wilczynski family lived at 2617 W. 16th Street on Chicago's west side. That area is called Pilsen, in honor of the town in what is now known as the Czech Republic. This

7

neighborhood was a common destination for the Eastern European immigrants.

The Czechs were famous for their robust beer. Pilsner Urquell is the Bohemian brew's name today. Ya know, I think I will stop writing and go have one right now. ....Mmmmm-boy, that was good! So, where was I?

Grampa Wilczynski was a very talented tailor. He crafted men's suits and other items of clothing for the well established B. Kupenheimer & Co. This was a skill that made it easy for the young couple to blend in to early 20th century Chicago. Agata played out her role as your garden-variety immigrant homemaker. Her skill set ran along the usual domestic lines of preparing sausage, carrots, potatoes and cabbage-based Polish fare, mopping floors, washboard scrubbing of soiled clothing and raising Catholic children, as well as raising her voice in order to get hubby John to help with the household chores. My mother inherited Agata's high decibel vocal prowess.

The wedding photo of my maternal grandparents.
Welcome if you will, Mr. and Mrs. John Wilczynski (applause).
Author's Collection

In 1873, an organization sprang up in Chicago known as the Polish Roman Catholic Union of America (PRCUA). To this day, it is *the* major fraternal organization established to assist Polish people yearning for freedom in their new country. The Union provided financial assistance, grants, scholarships and life insurance for the growing Polish community. John wasted no time. He traveled to the corner of Augusta and Milwaukee Avenues to sign up immediately upon his arrival in the New World. His PRCUA life insurance payout would come in handy for his lovely daughters a few years later.

Every once in a while, somewhere in the world, an inquisitive soul thirsty for knowledge, takes a sip of beer and asks "Why did all these Polish people come to America?" Good question! Poland had been a country under siege for centuries making it difficult for its citizens to establish a stable national identity. Its geographic location put it right smack dab in the middle of conflicts and uprisings with neighboring countries Russia, Lithuania, France, Germany and Austria. Let's just say Poland was the doormat for warring nations in the area much like, until 2016, the Chicago Cubs baseball team had been the doormat of the National League. The constant invasions, partitioning, religious and cultural suppression and the wars and rumors of war forced many to flee for a better life. The *"In America the streets are paved with gold"* mantra was reverberating throughout the highways and byways from Krakow to Gdansk. Chicago became the final destination for the largest Polish population outside of Warsaw.

The Eastern European expatriates brought many skills with them: carpentry, masonry, and the increasingly valuable talent for creating domestic beverages such as homemade beer, homemade basement wine, homemade garage vodka and the legendary "bath tub gin". This was a popular practice during the days of the highly unpopular 18th amendment to the U. S. Constitution that the average citizen knew as Prohibition. Of course, quality control was spotty at best. When his workday was done, John spent a little too much time sampling those homemade distilled spirits while offering his services as a neighborhood quality-control volunteer.

Let's review: the 18th amendment, technically known as the Volstead Act, was ratified on January 16, 1919 and went into effect one year later. It was a well-intentioned attempt to curtail the boozing up of America, the sinful sipping of suds and the wild wooing of women with wine, whiskey and song. The women's temperance movement and the Anti-Saloon League spearheaded this morality play. The ladies of the house wanted to assure domestic tranquility by keeping their hubbies and the wild party girls under control. Good luck with that one. Fuggedabowdit!

So, the wives wasted no time, hired a baby sitter, strapped on

9

their dropped waist-line party dresses and sparkling flapper beads and joined the fun. The roaring twenties began and roared-on in spite of populist efforts to squash the more base tendencies of the human condition. If there is a demand for a product or service, a capitalist somewhere will gladly fill all requests in exchange for the appropriate compensation.

A Hyde Park corner liquor store around 1910, advertising Pilsener beer on draught, Old Crow Whiskey and imported wines and liquors. After the Volstead act, they had to switch to fruits and vegetables.
Courtesy Special Collections Research Center, University of Chicago Library

In the early 20th century, Chicago was still rebuilding from the great fire of 1871 and corruption was rampant. There were some fond memories of great events such as the Columbian Exposition of 1893. Of course that world-class fair was tarnished by the devil-in-the-white-city, mass murderer H.H. Holmes. Lucky Chicago – home to America's first serial killer. To many outsiders, Chicago was a wide-open frontier town and a gritty manufacturing hub where jobs were plentiful. This attracted both skilled and unskilled workers from nations overseas as well as from the deep south in the USA. Hard working "birds of a feather" stuck together and created a city of ethnic neighborhoods, often divided along racial lines. This segregated "city of big shoulders", already home to about 2 million citizens, was in a relentless population boom. The Chicago city limits needed to expand. Neighboring towns were annexed one after another putting a strain on urban services especially law enforcement. As a result, the bad guys had an easy time evading the clutches of the men in blue. They pretty much ran the city with the official blessing of Mayor William Hale "Big Bill" Thompson.

Organized crime made sure booze flowed freely to the neighborhoods, to the rich and famous, to the speakeasies and to City Hall. Newspaper headlines constantly blared out exploits of the Northside Irish Dion "Deanie" O'Bannion gang (soon to be run by George "Bugs" Moran) and the Southside Johnny Torrio Italian crew (soon to be run by Al Capone). They generated serious cash flow selling illegal beverages to a thirsty partying populace letting loose after World War One. Naturally, many police were on the take. *"I would complain, but who would listen?"* Cops are human. They get thirsty too. Hey, they have a tough job! Eventually, it all became a zero-sum game. Prohibition was repealed by the 21st Amendment in 1933.

Meanwhile, back in the neighborhoods, down-to-earth family types were just trying to blend in, get a decent job, dodge bullets and raise a family. As you can imagine, things can get out of control with the media reporting so much vice busting out all around. On the home front, Agata took action when John's after-work partying became problematic as his happy hours unhappily degenerated into abuse. She filed for divorce shortly after my Aunt Helen was born in 1920.

One of Murphy's Laws states, *"Every solution breeds new problems"*. Separation and divorce created a new problem for my Gramma; financial hardship. She solved that one by sending the girls to a Catholic managed boarding school, the "Industrial School for Girls" in Des Plaines, Illinois. The school was founded in 1883 on 880 rolling acres just outside Chicago. It is now known as Maryville Academy.

Agata signed a contract on Nov 15, 1922. She agreed to pay $15 a month for each girl, a $45 total monthly obligation. Agata intentionally gave incorrect birth years for the three girls that made them appear one year older to circumvent the minimum age requirement at the school. The actual age of the girls at the time of their enrollment was 2, 4 and 6.

Trusting an institution to care for her progeny was risky. This temporary measure initially intended to allow Agata to "get over the hump" became an exceptionally long temporary measure. My mother and aunts stayed there for eleven years, which included 8 years of grammar school and all of those birthdays, Christmas days, Thanksgiving days, Easter Sundays, 4th-of-Julys and Halloweens. Overall, the children were treated well. Their health was never in jeopardy. In grammar school, they were normal average students with no disciplinary issues. For practical reasons, Florence and Stella were placed in the same grade. The record shows that Helen performed slightly better than her older siblings. In addition to classroom work, there was a hands-on working farm where the kids learned about gardening, crafts and basic hammer-meets-nail shop skills. Grampa John visited occasionally and kept in touch but Agata handled all legal, financial and medical issues (well...sort of).

11

School officials hounded Gramma for the entire eleven-year period trying to get her to pay up. She worked several jobs, including kitchen duty at the Glencoe Country Club, which enabled her to afford a car. That discovery really infuriated the school. Agata knew that boarding schools were not in the business of strapping juveniles into the ejection seat when parents failed to "please remit". Agata became a virtuoso at failing to "please remit." Gramma knew the girls would receive proper care so she tactfully avoided the payment issue. Ethically dubious: practically expedient. Naughty, naughty Gramma! As we shall see, somebody is setting a bad example for her kids, especially Florence.

In 1925, Grampa John became gravely ill. He eventually lost his life to acute catarrhal laryngitis. John had the foresight to take out a $1000 life insurance policy with his three daughters as beneficiaries. The PRCUA chipped in a death benefit of $500. The school was eventually paid off with that money.

Whoa, not so fast! Let's back up here. Enter into the story one, shall we say, less than totally honest Chicago lawyer. Robert E. Hogan had an office downtown at 105 W. Monroe Street. Highly experienced and well-known, Hogan specialized in family law. He was designated trustee of the insurance money when John's Last Will and Testament went to the Crook (sic) County probate court.

Shakespeare wrote an appropriate prologue to the Hogan situation:

"The first thing we do, let's kill all the lawyers. . . ."

Well guess what! The highly experienced well-known attorney Robert "The Robber" Hogan absconded with the insurance payout by depositing the $1000 check in his personal bank account. The life insurance money had been reserved for the boarding school in the name of the commandant, Father John Collins. Slick attorney Hogan forged Collins' signature. In due time, "Robber" Hogan was caught, disbarred and jailed. What was he thinking? These people don't live in a vacuum. Criminal minds are attracted to soft targets and easy money I guess.

Being the roaring twenties with the gangs and dirty politicians getting all the attention in the local press, perhaps Hogan thought he could fly under the proverbial radar and get away with a $1000 dollar rip off – a mere pittance when compared to the millions raked in by the outlaw factions of the day. Years later, the popular television series, *HOGAN'S HEROES*, featured a character, Colonel Robert E. Hogan. I doubt that character was named in memory of the highly experienced and street-wise attorney Hogan. But, who knows? Stranger things have happened. Rumor has it that our beloved cultural icon Bugs Bunny was named after the "Murder Incorporated" hit man and highly experienced

12

street-wise Las Vegas entrepreneur, Bugsy Siegel.

Let's be fair. Chicago wasn't all crooks, cronies and crazies during the 1920's and '30's. The Wilczynski girls were witnesses to many great things that were happening in technology. In 1921, the miracle of amplitude modulated radio began to weave its way into the fabric of American life. The first AM station was KYW, followed by iconic stations WGN, WLS, WMAQ and WCFL. The forerunner of Hizzonor Mayor Richard J. Daley, Hizzmajesty Mayor William Hale Thompson even had his own station, WHT. That made it pretty darned easy to get late night snacks and booze hand-delivered to city hall. Over on Grand Avenue, Giacomo's *House Of Pizza and Bootleg Beer* was commissioned to stay tuned in 24/7 to fill the Mayor's food and beverage orders.

Electronics firms Westinghouse, Zenith and Radio Corporation of America (RCA), could barely keep up with the demand for radios. These electronic squawk boxes became the centerpiece of homes across the nation. The orange glow of vacuum tube heater elements inside the radio fascinated both young and old. The burn-your-fingers-if-you-touch-them hot glass tubes provided warmth for the family kitty-cats luxuriating on top of beautifully crafted wooden consoles. The sound of music, variety shows, news and farm reports filled the living rooms of families who could afford this new luxury. Although not yet available to the general public, rumors of another miraculous electronic invention stirred the imagination. This time, electronics engineers came up with a box crammed with tubes, capacitors, resistors, tuned inductors and wires that could receive both sound *and* pictures. This novelty was called *television*. The film industry, Hollywood's magic movie machine, feared that this latest thing would put them out of business. That apparently did not happen. After we get those movie machine magicians to make the story in this book into an exciting motion picture "based on true events", they can go ahead and shut down, call it a day and happy trails to you.

Chicago Industrial School for Girls

Des Plaines, Cook County, Illinois

I hereby agree to pay to Chicago Industrial School for Girls a corporation of the State of Illinois, and located at Des Plaines, Illinois, in advance, on the first day of each and every month, from the date hereof until this contract is terminated as herein provided, the sum of _____ *Forty-five* _____ Dollars, for the care, board and tuition of *Stella — Florence — Helen Wilczyska* hereinafter referred to as the Said Boarder;

I further hereby agree to furnish or supply the said Boarder with all such books, clothing, etc., which the School Management may deem necessary for the well being of the said Boarder;

I also further hereby agree to reimburse Chicago Industrial School for Girls for all books, clothing, medical care and attention, dental work, or for any other special service which the said School may supply, furnish, provide or perform for the said Boarder; provided, however, that any such expense is incurred with my consent.

I agree to indemnify and save harmless Chicago Industrial School for Girls from all liability on account of any accident, resulting in the injury to or death of the said Boarder, occurring while the said Boarder is in the care and custody of the said School.

This contract may be terminated at any time by either of the parties hereto.

Dated at Des Plaines, Illinois, _____ *Nov. 15* 1922

Accepted:

Chicago Industrial School for Girls

_____
Manager

_____
Signature of Parent or Guardian

Gramma Agata Wilczynski signed this contract with
the boarding school on November 15, 1922.
Author's Collection

14

Aunt Helen Wilczynski with an unnamed priest at
the boarding school in Des Plaines Illinois.
This picture is from 1923 when Helen was 3 years old.
Author's Collection

June 7, 1928.

Mrs. Agnes Wilczynski,
C/o Mrs. A. Kogut,
5047 Cullom Ave.,
Chicago, Ill.

My Dear Mrs. Wilczynski:

Has anyone from the Juvenile Court
been to see you regarding the children? Is anything being
done in the matter, do you know. If not, I wish you would
keep after them. They are very slow in these matters, and,
as I explained to you personally, something must be done
soon for the bill is mounting up and the way it looks I
fear there is little likelihood of collecting on that insurance.

Have you been to Mr. Hogan's office since I saw
you last. If not, wish you would make it your business to
see him soon and endeavor to find out whether or not they
have located that insurance policy and if anything can be
collected on it.

I am quite sure your intentions are the best and
that you want our school to be treated rightly in the matter,
and this is one way you can help by going after both the
Juvenile Court and Mr. Hogan's office to get the matter
straightened out.

Call me some morning, or in the evening, even if
as late as between 10 and 10:30 and you will be almost sure
to get me. My 'phone now is ~~Radcliffe 5877. Address,
7808 Indiana Ave., 1st floor.~~

Awaiting to hear from you as soon as possible, I
am

Sincerely yours,

Visitor.

A letter to Gramma from 1928 mentions attorney Hogan. It had not
yet been discovered that Hogan stole the $1000.00 insurance check.
The boarding school was sounding as if they were just about ready
to give up on the thought of ever collecting what was owed.
But, like my aunt Stella always said, "Better days are coming".

Author's Collection

Chicago Industrial School for Girls

Des Plaines, Cook County, Illinois

Aug. 2, 1929.

Mrs. Agnes Wilczynski,
C/o Mrs. A. Kogut,
5047 Cullom Ave.,
Chicago.

Dear Mrs. Wilczynski:

I called up the Wittbold Floral Co. to-day and was told you had quit your position there a week ago last Tuesday. I am wondering why. I am also wondering how you will ever meet the payments on the automobile you purchased recently. Besides, it will be absolutely necessary that you meet $45.00 a month from now for as long as your girls remain at St. Mary's

By the way, did you mention to Father Collins the fact that you had paid nearly three hundred dollars down on an automobile and contracted to pay $37.00 a month for the balance--while all the while your children are being supported on charity. Have you forgotten that there is some $1100.00 or over due right now? Should a woman in your position in life own a machine?

I had believed you were on the square with us, but I regret to say I have changed my mind. I can hardly conceive of a mother with three small children without any other means but what you earn in a kitchen running around the city in an automobile of her own. I could use one very nicely in my business but I cannot afford it.

Well, you have lost all my sympathy and I shall from now use every endeavor to see that you pay regularly for your children or else take them home. The matter anyhow is in the hands of the Juvenile Court and the Court no doubt will see to it that you do your duty from now on.

Yours very truly,

_____
Visitor.

NTS
Home: 7008 Indiana Ave.
Radcliffe 5077.

P. S. I believe that your sister, Mrs. Kogut, would be glad to take the children. If you do not want to take care of them why not let her have them. This is probably what the court will compel you to do if you do not do your part as a mother.

In this August 2nd letter, the boarding school lets Gramma have it. They did not mince words accusing her of being able to afford a car while ignoring her financial obligation for her daughters' care.

Author's Collection

17

My Father, Walter Stanley Baran

My paternal grandparents were also both Polish immigrants. Josef Baran was born in Biała Wisniowa on July 19, 1884. He arrived in Chicago in 1901. Sofie Pozdol was born May 15, 1882, in Stara Jastrzabka and came to America in 1902. Josef and Sofie met in Chicago and were married at St. Ann's Catholic Church in 1906.

Josef was no slacker. He was a hard working reliable man employed as a binder inspector for a farm machinery manufacturer, the McCormick Reaper Works later known as International Harvester at 22nd Street and Western Avenue. Sofie stayed home, baked cakes and cookies and started popping out little first-generation American-born Polish babies.

My father, Walter, born November 15th, 1910 was the 2nd oldest of five. His siblings were; oldest sister Anna born 1908, Frank 1912, Helen 1916, and Edward ("*hey Uncle Eddie, pour me a high ball*") born 1919.

Josef worked hard, saved his money and bought the building they lived in. This was a three-flat on Chicago's near south side at 1851 West 20th Street, about a mile from where the Wilczynskis lived. There is no record that these families knew each other at the time.

Grampa had two tenants in the building providing income to assist in paying the mortgage – smart move. They also had a family friend, a boarder Stella Slirkewicz, who helped with the bills. From all indications, Mr. Josef Baran was a shrewd money manager. So *that's* where my dad learned that.

Grampa Baran died suddenly of a stroke May 28th, 1927 and was laid to rest at Resurrection Cemetery near Chicago. Sofie was left with the five kids and never remarried.

Walter left school after sixth grade and found work wherever he could. Along the way, he learned some basic carpentry skills and put them to practical use. Dad once showed me a large sturdy wooden toolbox that he had built as a teenager. He kept it around for many years. Together with his brothers, Eddie and Frank, he built a garage behind the three story apartment building where they moved shortly after Grampa Josef's death. That garage at 2541 W. 39th Place in Chicago, is still there. It now sports new doors, windows and updated siding.

It's unfortunate that both of my parents spent many of their formative years without a father in the picture. However, compared to Florence, Walter's early life was much less complicated. He had family and relatives around while Flo had priests, nuns and other civilian strangers as role models and confidants.

My Grandfather Josef Baran (standing) and
Grandmother Sofie Pozdol (standing left) with
unidentified friends.
Author's Collection

Young Walter Baran at his Catholic Confirmation.
Dad was stylin' with those short pants and hi-top shoes!
It would be interesting to know what year this picture was taken.
Author's Collection

The Bandit, William "Bill" Howard Gaskell

Bill's father, Howard William Gaskell Sr. was born in Wisconsin in 1872. His parents both hailed from Scotland. Bill's mother Agnes Wills was born in Chicago in May, 1893. Her father was of German descent and her mother emigrated from Ireland.

Howard and Agnes were married in Chicago on Sep 13, 1919. For some reason, they moved to Canton Ohio that year, maybe for employment or possibly to escape the shame of the 1919 World Series Black Sox scandal (ha ha ha just kidding). They were guests of the John Kile family at 2415 Fourteenth Street. Howard was an ironworker, a skill in great demand in rust belt Ohio. The young couple soon moved back to Chicago and started making babies. Enter three cute little baby Gaskells.

Bandit Bill was born Howard William Gaskell Jr on January 12, 1927, the youngest of three. His older brother Lawrence (born 1921) and sister Eileen (born 1923) rounded out the sibling count. The 1930 census has the family living at 3042 North Leavitt on Chicago's northwest side Avondale neighborhood. Howard Sr. leaned on his skill as an ironworker and found employment with a local manufacturer, the then-famous Henry C. Grebe boat company. It was located at the intersection of Belmont Avenue and the north branch of the Chicago River, a short walk from the Gaskell home. With the Great Depression in full swing, Howard Sr. was lucky to have a job.

However, Howard Jr. howled about the name Howard. Much to his father's dismay and with the blessing from momma Agnes, junior eventually reversed his middle and first name to become William Howard Gaskell. After a few years, once again with momma's approval, he would change his name in order to perpetrate enlistment fraud against the United States Navy during WW II. We'll get into that later.

More detailed information about the Gaskell's early family life has been hard to find. I was lucky enough to track down as much as I have. You're not getting bored with this are you? Look at their cool family picture on the next page.

21

The Gaskells pose at their home on Chicago's NW side, 1931.
In the window L-R, Bill's brother Lawrence (10), momma Agnes (39)
and sister Eileen (8). Billy (4), yawning Sparky dog and Howard Sr. (53)
relax in the foreground. If you look closely, you can see two little horns
growing out of little Billy's head. I see trouble on the horizon.
Author's Collection

GROWING UP IN CHICAGO

Walter and Florence, children of Polish immigrants would soon meet. Their lives together started with great promise and idealism. As time went on, the union would show signs of discontent and frustration. Across town, the bandit's young life was heading in a completely different direction. The clearly disparate circumstances surrounding their upbringing led them down some long dusty roads that met at a junction none of them could have predicted. But first, they all had some growing up to do.

The Wilczynski Girls Free At Last

After eleven years at the Des Plaines boarding school, Florence, Stella and Helen went home to live with mother Agata. In June of 1933, Helen was 13, Florence 15 and Stella 17. They first settled in Chicago's Hyde Park neighborhood above a store at 5462 S. Lake Park Avenue right across the street from the Illinois Central 55th Street station. This was a bustling area left over from the 1893 Columbian Exposition. It was crowded with multi-use mostly wooden structures of shops, apartments and taverns. Not exactly an ideal place to raise kids but sometimes a single mom must take what she can get and make the best of it. The nice thing was the close proximity to schools, Jackson Park, the 57th Street beach and the newly opened Museum of Science and Industry.

The Wilczynski girls were free at last and beginning a new life. The giggling fun-loving trio were treated to the beginning of another great event, the 1933 Chicago World's Fair, known as The Century of Progress. Like the 1893 Columbian Exposition, the fair was on Chicago's scenic lakefront. This was within walking distance of where the girls lived. If that wasn't enough fun, major league baseball's first All-Star game was played at Comiskey Park, then the home of the Chicago White Sox. This was great news for Flo who was a big baseball fan and a good athlete. She was a strong young gal, fired up and ready for action. The summer of 1933 was going to be fun in the sun for the girls.

The decade of the thirties produced some wonderful songs that crackled over the AM radio dial. Flo and her sisters waltzed away the hours humming and singing along with the hits of the day like "Putting On The Ritz" and "The Way You Look Tonite" (Fred Astaire), "It Don't Mean A Thing If It Ain't Got That Swing" (Duke Ellington), "Thanks For The Memories" (Bob Hope), "When You Wish Upon A Star" (Cliff Edwards) and "Somewhere Over The Rainbow" (Judy Garland).

In September 1933, Gramma enrolled Florence and Helen at the all-girl St. Thomas the Apostle High School. The school records are blank except for their name and address. They never attended classes since Gramma could not afford the tuition. She didn't need to go through another financial "catch-me-if-you-can" like before in Des Plaines. The alternative was public school. The girls attended Hyde Park Public High School at 62nd and Stony Island. Helen finished her junior year and Florence made it through her sophomore year and then went right to work. This was in the middle of the Great Depression of the 1930's. The girls needed to help with family finances any way they could. Cute little Helen found work waiting tables at a neighborhood restaurant.

Aunt Stella agreed that a waitress gig at a Hyde Park restaurant was more fun than school. Bypassing any further education, she also waited tables and soon could afford a small apartment at 5610 S. Dorchester. There she met her longtime boyfriend, George Livermore. They were listed as tenants in the 1940 census.

About 1937, Florence found herself serving vegetable and fruit drinks at a health food restaurant in downtown Chicago. Walter toiled there stocking shelves and managing incoming supplies. This was Bossow's Health Food Store and Restaurant at 19 East Van Buren Street. Walter and Florence met there and began a casual relationship.

Dad recalled that it was managed by a famous pioneering health food advocate of the time. Wally was a big fan of this man and others of the same persuasion. Young Walter endured painful digestive ailments during those years. Given our modern take on these things, Wally might have been lactose intolerant or suffered from a gluten allergy or both. As a result, he became totally obsessed with dietary issues.

Gramma Sofie would regularly feed him and his four siblings, cream puffs, donuts, cakes and Polish pastries. Sounds like fun comfort food. Florence recalled that before they met, Walter was hospitalized for an emotional disorder or some physical ailment. She could not remember exactly what the problem was and, of course, in later years, we couldn't talk to our dad about those things. If we did, Walter would have just ignored our inquiry followed by a firm command to "Eat this seaweed. There's iodine in there!" Seaweed good! Cream puffs bad!

Playful Aunt Helen hovers over Florence circa 1933
Author's Collection

Flo and Helen again with unidentified friend.
Swimsuit modeling was apparently on the agenda.
Author's Collection

After discovering carrot juice, Wally had an epiphany. He began his life-long crusade to convert his family and friends to the alternative diet of whole wheat bread, fish, raw peanuts and almonds, wheat germ, kelp, dulce powder, fruit juices, vegetable juice and.... well, you get the idea. Everything not specifically mentioned on his approved list was summarily tagged as junk food.

Young Walter was convinced his diet was synonymous with medicine, a natural cure for his numerous maladies. He spent hours reading books by nutrition experts of the time. Always skeptical, dad once posed the question to a pharmacist: "Just what is a drug?" As far as he was concerned, the medical establishment in general and doctors in particular, were quacks at worst and misinformed at best. He often claimed that he knew more about healthy living than most doctors. Perhaps he did. One could say he was ahead of his time on some level. For better or for worse, he was unyieldingly black and white on the issue of diet. One author stood out in dad's mind. This "foodie" of great repute had a huge influence on Walter. Apparently, this man was no flash-in-the-pan wild-haired bulging-eyed street-corner-soap-box-weirdo fanatic. He was nothing like me for sure.

Lelord Kordel (1904 – 2001) was a Polish American nutritionist and author of many books on healthy living, diet and exercise. Born in Warsaw, Poland, Kordel emigrated with his parents to the United States as a child and grew up in Chicago, where his father worked as a baker. After university studies in Chicago, Kordel returned to Poland to continue his education at the University of Krakow earning a Ph.D. in biochemistry in 1930. He worked for two years as a science instructor and then took up a position as a research assistant to a British physician, Sir William Arbuthnot-Lane, whose theories influenced his career as a nutritionist.

Back in the USA, Lelord became a health food researcher and industry consultant. Kordel developed programs for healthy living and pioneered concepts for dietary supplementation. During the 1940's, he conducted and supervised seminars on nutrition for the war effort and was a prime mover in the "*Food and Nutrition for Victory*" programs, for which he earned many awards. After the war, Kordel authored books on health and nutrition. His most well known book, "*Eat and Grow Younger*" (1952) sold over 4 million copies. It is still sought out today. Kordel followed his own advice and lived to 97. So, Walter had his Polish hero and role model and was all-in. *Junk food be damned!* Florence was at the opposite end of the dietary spectrum. In later years, this was to become a major divisive domestic issue.

Walter And Florence Get Married

Walter Stanley Baran and Florence Mary Wilczynski (now shortened to Wills) exchanged marriage vows at St. Joseph and St Anne's Catholic Church. This was at the corner of California and 38th Place in Chicago's Brighton Park Neighborhood. The parish is now called Our Lady of Fatima.

The marriage certificate shows that the *then* happy couple entered into the "Holy Bonds of Matrimony" on Monday, February 29th, 1938. Someone entered the wrong date. February 29th, the so-called "leap day", occurs only in leap years. Leap years of that era were 1936 and 1940. Another church record shows the nuptials occurred on Saturday, February 26th 1938. That was probably correct. Wally and Flo got off to a bad start?

Excerpt from the 1940 census. The young couple rented
an apartment at 2628 W 21st Street. It shows Walter as "Head" of the
family, Florence is the "Wife" and their first born daughter Nancy.
Author's Collection

Certificate of Marriage

I, the undersigned, do hereby certify, that on the *29th* day of *February* A.D. 19*38* in the church of *St. Joseh & Anne* I joined in the

Holy Bonds of Matrimony

Walter Baran and *Florence Wills*

according to the rites of the Holy Roman Catholic Church.

Witness: *Frank Baran*
Helen Wills   *P. F. De Salles*

It is a beautiful marriage certificate. Unfortunately, someone didn't know their leap year from a crock of czernina.

Author's Collection

Mr. and Mrs. Walter Baran stroll out of St. Joseph and St Anne's
Catholic Church just moments after exchanging vows.
The expression "the calm before the storm" comes to mind.
The next 50 years would be an adventure of Biblical proportions.
Author's Collection

The newlyweds flanked by my uncle Frank Baran and
Aunt Helen Wills. That is one beautiful wedding dress, yes?
Florence was living her romantic dream. Walter never suspected
that his teenage bride had been secretly raised by Tasmanian Devils.
Author's Collection

Smiles all around except for the always stoic Gramma Sofie (standing).
She hosted the marriage banquet in her apartment living room
on the third floor at 2541 W. 39th Place, Chicago.
Aunt Helen is left of Wally and Aunt Stella is on the far right.
Gramma Agata is seated next to Gramma Baran.
Author's Collection

The happy couple got right down to the important business of procreation, propagation of the species, proliferation of the Polish ethnicity, reserving dates to fecundate and the begetting of the Barans. In other words, they decided to have children. On December 23, 1938, almost exactly nine months after the wedding, my big sis Nancy was born. Meanwhile, Hitler and his German military machine were planning the invasion of Poland and had their beady little Nazi eyes on Czechoslovakia and the rest of Eastern Europe. More storm clouds were forming on the horizon, not only in Europe and in the west Pacific, but right here at home in Chicago.

Ma Flo (L), aunt Helen and Nancy, early 1939. Ma wore a proud
mother's smile while Nancy stared into the blue sky dreaming about her
next meal of warm and creamy all-natural mother's milk.
Author's Collection

A smiling first-time dad in spring 1939, flanked by two relatives.
Bashful Nancy hides behind daddy's hand.
Sorry for the blurred pic.
Author's Collection

By the time Florence came home with the baby, my Ma and Pa had already decided that their marriage was a mistake. 9 months of daily contentious combative quarreling punctuated with mean-spirited name-calling was long enough. Just like oil and water, Wally's carrot juice and Flo's cookies didn't mix. Just in the nick of time, Gramma Sofie intervened. Acting as marriage counselor from God, she urged them to stay married for the child's sake. Hmmm, is that ever a good idea? In those days, divorce was relatively rare. Couples worked together just to survive. This was especially true during the Great Depression. Okay. So they held their noses and stuck it out. We'll see how that plan worked.

The Gaskell Family

In the early 1930's, Howard and Agnes packed up the three kids, Lawrence, Eileen and Howard Jr. and moved to Oklahoma. This was during the Great Depression that included those nasty dust bowl years. Howard must have had a compelling reason to take the family out of the big city and plop them down in Oklahoma in the middle of such desperate times. Since daddy was a skilled ironworker, he possibly landed an oil field gig or found a WPA job.

FYI: Of all of President Roosevelt's New Deal programs, the Works Progress Administration (WPA) is the most famous, because it affected so many Americans across the country. Roosevelt's vision of the depression-easing work-relief program employed more than 8.5 million people. For an average salary of $41.57 a month, WPA employees built bridges, roads, public buildings, public parks and airports.

In March of 1935, Agnes and Howard separated. Maybe her constant complaining about all the dust in the morning oatmeal finally got to Howard. She was an ardent city girl and longed for the familiar surroundings of hometown Chicago. They were not on the same page. Howard soon sued Agnes for divorce citing abandonment. Agnes contested the charge of abandonment and accused Howard of the same. Their divorce action bounced around the Oklahoma court system for several years. Agnes eventually granted Howard divorce after many appeals.

At some point during all this, Agnes packed up the kids, left Howard in the dust, and moved back to Chicago. She settled in Hyde Park finding an apartment in one of the historic grey stone two-flats that were typical of Chicago's south side. This was at 5550 S. Drexel just down the street from the prestigious University of Chicago. When sixteen year-old Bill applied for his Social Security card a few years later, he used that address.

It soon became clear that Bill needed a strong disciplinarian around. The Rascal Billy Gaskell was in his formative period. Without a positive male role model to guide him, he instinctively looked for some one to emulate.

In later years, Bill shared an apartment with his mom
at 5230 S Lake Park. This building was built during
the housing boom of the 1890's in Hyde Park and
disappeared during the urban renewal of the 1960's.
Courtesy Special Collections Research Center, University of Chicago Library

Given all that followed in the 1940's and '50's, one could
successfully wager that Bill assumed the persona of Rocky Sullivan, a
fictional character played to the hilt by famed actor, James Cagney. The
3-time Oscar nominated film, "Angels With Dirty Faces" was a major hit
released to the movie theaters in 1938, just in time for Bill's 11th
birthday. It's the story of two young boys growing up in the Hell's
Kitchen neighborhood of New York City. Rocky's buddy, Jerry
Connolly, was played by another Hollywood legend, Pat O'Brien. They
get into big trouble together, and do time in reform school. Rocky
sharpens his criminal skills there and evolves into a stick-up artist and
short-tempered street thug. This tough guy act lands him doing hard time
in the big house. Connolly takes the opposite path and becomes a priest
in the old neighborhood, dedicating his life to the task of keeping local
youth on the straight and narrow. They meet again years later when

Rocky is released from prison. The story continues with Humphrey Bogart making an appearance, as well as Leo Gorcey and the Dead End Kids. According to Bill's ex-wife, there was a lot of Rocky Sullivan in Billy Gaskell.

Another influence on Bill was his brother Lawrence. Six years older, he grew up challenging the status quo with his own tough guy act. Big brother spent years in and out of the penitentiary and eventually took his permanent dirt nap in a pauper's grave. Bill looked up to big brother and wanted to be just like him. The record shows that Bill succeeded.

In the 1930's, there was a movie theater called *The Frolic*. It was at 951 E. 55th Street, two short blocks from the Gaskells. Like a good momma should, Agnes regularly treated the kids to first run movies of the time like *Gone With The Wind* and *The Wizard Of Oz*. It's easy to see that the Cagney movie and other big screen crime dramas of the era could have fired up Bill's young, pliable and impressionable imagination. One day, he must have been daydreaming out loud; *"I wonder what a cold steel pistol would feel like in my young, pliable and impressionable right hand."* He would soon get his chance to find out. Young Bill was now programmed to travel the path that would lead to living by his own moral code outside society's norms. He aligned himself with the scofflaws and outlaws darkening the doorways of cellblocks from sea to shining sea. Sometimes they live a good life. Sometimes they just wind up dead in an alley. For many, it was loads of fun while it lasted.

The Frolic Theater was just off the corner at the right.
Courtesy Special Collections Research Center, University of Chicago Library

37

The Housewife Loved a Bandit – Chapter 4
LIFE DURING WORLD WAR II TIME

"Praise the Lord and pass the whole wheat bread"

Walter and Florence Baran, Husband, Wife and Family

September 1, 1939, Hitler attacked Poland. This ushered in what some people have called the second "war-to-end-all-wars", the war fought and won by the "Greatest Generation". But, Walter had his medical problems. With his history of gastrointestinal ailments and some depression issues, he was classified 4F.

No self-respecting gals would date the boys who didn't pass their physicals. Those fellas were called "4-Fers." This classification was given primarily for muscular and bone malformations, hearing or circulatory ailments, mental deficiency, disease, hernias and syphilis. Everybody else was going off to war. The ones left behind were often considered "slackers". Hey, come on now you self-righteous finger-pointers, back off. Someone has to stay home and build the ships, bombs and Jeeps. And what about all those lonely women and "Rosey the Riveter" types? *"Hey there big boy, could you spare a minute to show me how to light my oxy-acetylene torch, you big brute you?"* You just gotta love a graceful grinning gal wistfully waving a 5000 degree welding tool! R-E-S-P-E-C-T!

Flat feet and punctured eardrums were other ailments that excused men from military service. "Flat feet" meant fallen arches, which a manly man could pretty much live with back home on the block, but would make it difficult to complete a 20-mile forced march with full combat gear. "Punctured eardrums" were something most of these men didn't know they had until an Army doctor broke the news. *"So that's why I couldn't hear my wife's bitching and moaning. Oh, Sorry dear. I didn't think you were listening."*

According to the 1940 US Census, the young Baran family leased a cold water flat at 2628 W. 21st street. Walter paid $14 a month rent. They shared this six-flat building with other families with names like Vidmar, Glyzewski and Ruczko.

FYI: A cold water flat is an apartment that has no running hot water. In most developed countries, modern building codes list cold water flats as illegal. Throughout the early twentieth century, they were very common in cities such as Detroit and Chicago. In general, cold-water flats did not have showers. If tenants wanted to bathe, they would heat pots of water on their cooking stove. Once the water reached a rolling boil, it was important to avoid tripping over the family cat while carrying the steaming caldron to daddy's bath.

These apartments usually had no central heating system. The working class tenants would keep warm by wearing layers of sweaters, huddling around space heaters fueled by kerosene, electricity, coal, or by hugging large furry dogs. Shivering Florence was not happy about having to constantly deal with their coal-fired space heater. This was not a joyous and romantic period for the young couple. Ma was getting cranky but found one way to escape her predicament. She got into the habit of singing while she washed dishes, something she did well into later life. She would close her eyes, smile and sing with great feeling. You could tell she really loved it. Some of her favorites of the era were "Sentimental Journey", "White Christmas", "Swinging on a Star", "Zip A Dee Doo Dah", "You Are My Sunshine", "Rudolph The Red-Nosed Reindeer" and "The Christmas Song".

The Barans survived the cold-water-flat era eventually welcoming sisters Jeanne (May 1940) and Loretta (July 1942) and brother Frederick James (September 1944). Apparently, Wally and Flo found one way to keep nice and warm.

During this time, Walter worked in President Roosevelt's WPA program. My dad was a laborer doing odd jobs with the work crews that built Chicago's Lake Shore Drive southern extension to 47th Street. He became well acquainted with the basic tools of road construction such as pick axes, shovels, wheelbarrows and beer. After the Outer Drive project was finished, Wally found the job that would keep him supplied with his treasured health foods for the rest of his days.

Health Food Jobbers was a vitamin and food distributor located just south of Chicago's Loop on Clinton Street near Harrison. This was definitely Wally's World. He toiled faithfully as a shipping clerk handling both outgoing and incoming packages. Employees often intercepted damaged returned goods and, with the permission of the powers-that-be, brought them home to help feed their families. Eureka! Dad discovered gold! Everything his nutrition guru taught him was now at his fingertips. *"The whiter the bread, the sooner you're dead"* was a common catchphrase used by the health food and granola crowd. Meanwhile, Florence was still strapped into her role as stay-at-home mom. She was getting restless and crankier.

Gramma Agata still lived in Hyde Park leasing a garden apartment in a small house at 5466 S. Dorchester. She was always concerned about relatives left behind in Poland. It was particularly unsettling hearing about the war machine revving up in Europe. Right about this time, Agata legally shortened her married name from Wilczynski to Wills although her girls were already using it. She may have done this to avoid American prejudice against foreigners, or simply to make it easier for folks to pronounce and spell her last name. Wilczynski was a mouthful to some. That cluster of consonants, common to the Polish language, has always been a challenge for the uninitiated. How do *you* pronounce Zbigniew Rybczynski?

Gramma Wills with Aunt Helen about 1940. Now that the girls were all grown up, Gramma could afford stylish fashions.
Author's Collection

In 1945, Flo, Wally and the four kids, with a fifth on the way, squeezed into a three-room apartment at 5463 S Dorchester. The locals called that four-story 1890's slum-ish structure "The Misery Mansion". Cramming six Barans into three rooms called for some creative space planning. The move from the 21st street cold water flat was made, in part, to be closer to the family baby sitter, Gramma Wills who lived right across the street.

The Mansion supplied central heat from hot water radiators. This was definitely a step up from the heat-it-yourself drudgery on 21st street. The only real downside of this move was the high incidence of hooliganism in the area. In general, Hyde Park was a nice place to live, but that particular block and the immediate area had a high concentration of problem children contributing to the local crime stats.

Looking SE on Dorchester in the 1940's. "The Misery Mansion" looms
large complete with young toughs hangin' around looking for trouble.
Courtesy Special Collections Research Center, University of Chicago Library

  Alice Boarman, a family friend of seven decades, recalls racial
harassment by the young toughs who used the block as their hang out. Of
course, being Polish, there were shouts of "DP" and "babushka heads"
from the young slugs in the 'hood. Public transportation was great.
Several bus routes and the Illinois Central train stop just blocks away
made for an easy commute to any part of the big city. The nearby
beaches, parks and museum made it a decent place to raise kids.

  Aunt Stella still lived a short two blocks from the Mansion and
helped with baby-sitting. Aunt Helen, however, had moved on. She loved
to dress up like her idols, Lauren Bacall and Ann Sheridan. She dreamed
of stardom on the silver screen like so many young women of the time.
At some point, Helen ventured to Hollywood looking for a path into the
glitz and glamour of big screen stardom. She hoped her pretty face would
open a door and get her noticed. She found her way to a meet-and-greet
with two major stars of the day, romantic leading man Cesar Romero and
the Brazilian Bombshell Carmen Miranda. Given the evidence, this was
probably on the set of the 1941 movie *Weekend in Havana.* Carmen wore
that same colorful "hat" when she sang, romped and writhed to the tune
Rebola a Bola. You can watch it in living color on YouTube.

Aunt Helen (L), attends a 1940's Hollywood meet-and-greet with
6'3" Cesar Romero and 5' Carmen Miranda
Author's Collection

      That chance meeting with such major celebs of the day, triggered a bit of sibling rivalry between Flo and Helen. This would surface again in later years when Flo responded to the call of the wild in 1953. Ultimately, acting fame would elude Aunt Helen but she would eventually snare a small but important role in the exciting real life adventures of Flo and Bill. We are lucky that picture survived the decades as the silent witness to Helen's brush with fame.

      While still in California, Helen met a man from Bangor, Michigan. Ross Paul Hawthorne and Helen married in Hollywood on July 16, 1942. Everyone back home was surprised with that news. They honeymooned there in Southern California and came back to the Midwest in the fall. Another surprise announcement soon followed. Ross joined the Army on November 30, 1942.

      After the war, the Hawthornes moved to Michigan, settling briefly in Paw Paw and then finally in Kalamazoo. Soon after arriving in Kazoo, Helen took up acting in Community Theater. Ross was not on board with the wife's thespian activities. Their relationship turned sour. The union lasted until 1957 when Helen was granted a divorce citing mental cruelty. Years later, the Michigan connection became a vital part of this story.

Aunt Helen and Bangor Michigan's Ross Hawthorne 1943
Author's Collection

Professional portrait of Aunt Stella Wills circa 1940.
Nice smile there Stella.
Author's Collection

Aunt Stella's goals were much more down-to-earth. She just liked to hang out, grow tomatoes and listen to music. Her boyfriend, George Livermore, was born to American parents in Havana Cuba in 1911. He was a salesman of electrical equipment requiring him to travel from city to city for weeks at a time. His wife had passed away several years earlier. The lonely widower had found a nice girlfriend.

They shared use of a WW II army surplus Jeep. When George had to travel for business, Stella had the jeep all to herself. Stella could grind those gears with the best of them. She would thrill us kids with trips down Highway 41 to visit the Indiana dunes for summer days of frolicking in the sand. Stella eventually gave up her apartment and moved back in with Gramma at 5625 S Dorchester. After all those boarding school years, she graduated into a simple peaceful life. Our favorite aunt would later play a significant role in the exciting adventures of Flo and Bill.

Aunt Stella and boyfriend George Livermore, 1946,
relaxing at Jackson Park in their WW2 Army surplus Jeep
Author's Collection

Aunt Stella at the wheel with smiling Florence and three of my sisters.
Stella's doggie Mitzie served as a hood ornament.
Big tall Nancy better sit down or she'll wind up performing a
backwards summersault when Stella pops the clutch.
Author's Collection

Wally takes the wheel with Freddie in his lap while
Flo consoles an upset Loretta seated in back.
Author's Collection

TRIPLICATE
(To be given to declarant
when originally issued; to be
made a part of the petition
for naturalization when petition is filed; and to be re-
tained as part of the petition
in the records of the court)

UNITED STATES OF AMERICA

DECLARATION OF INTENTION
(Invalid for all purposes seven years after the date hereof)

No. 192594

UNITED STATES OF AMERICA
NORTHERN DISTRICT OF ILLINOIS } ss:

In the **DISTRICT** Court

of **THE UNITED STATES, CHICAGO,**

(1) My full, true, and correct name is **HELEN AGATA WILLS**

(2) My present place of residence is **5625 Dorchester Avenue** (3) My occupation is **Vegetable cook**

(4) I am **44** years old. (5) I was born on **Feb.5,1898** in **Kobylec,Poland**

(6) My personal description is as follows: Sex **female** color **white** complexion **fair** color of eyes **blue**
color of hair **d.brown** height **5** feet **3½** inches, weight **167** pounds, visible distinctive marks **None**
race **white**, present nationality **Polish**

(7) I am **widow**; the name of my wife or husband is **was John** ; we were married on **9/6/14**
at **Chicago, Ill** ; he or she was born at **Poland**
on **1898** and entered the United States at **New York, N.Y.**
on **1913** for permanent residence in the United States, and now resides at **Deceased 1925**

(8) I have **3** children; and the name, sex, date and place of birth, and present place of residence of each of said children who is living, are as follows:
Stella(F) 3/7/16 Florence(F) 3/30/18 Helen(F) 1/16/20.
All born in and reside in Chicago, Illinois

(9) My last place of foreign residence was **Copenhagen,Denmark** (10) I emigrated to the United States from
Liverpool, England (11) My lawful entry for permanent residence in the United States was
at **New York, N.Y** under the name of **Kwarciak,Agata**
on **Jan.5, 1911** on the **SS St. Paul**

(12) Since my lawful entry for permanent residence I have **not** been absent from the United States, for a period or periods of 6 months or longer, as follows:

DEPARTED FROM THE UNITED STATES			RETURNED TO THE UNITED STATES		
Port	Date (Month, day, year)	Vessel or other means of conveyance	Port	Date (Month, day, year)	Vessel or other means of conveyance

(13) I have **lost** heretofore made declaration of intention: No. **Superior or Circuit** on **1917** at
Chicago, Ill. in the **(State of court)**

(14) It is my intention in good faith to become a citizen of the United States and to reside permanently therein. (15) I will, before being admitted to citizenship, renounce absolutely and forever all allegiance and fidelity to any foreign prince, potentate, state, or sovereignty of whom or which at the time of admission to citizenship I may be a subject or citizen. (16) I am not an anarchist; nor a believer in the unlawful damage, injury, or destruction of property, or sabotage; nor a disbeliever in or opposed to organized government; nor a member of or affiliated with any organization or body of persons teaching disbelief in or opposition to organized government. (17) I certify that the photograph affixed to the duplicate and triplicate hereof is a likeness of me and was signed by me.
I do swear (affirm) that the statements I have made and the intentions I have expressed in this declaration of intention subscribed by me are true to the best of my knowledge and belief: SO HELP ME GOD.

Helen Agata Wills

Subscribed and sworn to (affirmed) before me in the form of oath shown above in the office of the Clerk of said Court, at **Chicago, Illinois**
this **9th** day of **July** anno Domini 19**42**. hereby certify that Certification No. **11-335471** from the Commissioner of Immigration and Naturalization, showing the lawful entry for permanent residence of the declarant above named on the date stated in this declaration of intention, has been received by me, and that the photograph affixed to the duplicate and triplicate hereof is a likeness of the declarant.

[SEAL]

HOYT KING
U.S. DISTRICT.
Clerk of the Court.
By *Zita M Keaney* Deputy Clerk.

Helen Agata Wills

Form N-315
U. S. DEPARTMENT OF JUSTICE
IMMIGRATION AND NATURALIZATION SERVICE
(Edition of 1-13-41)

Gramma Agata's Declaration Of Intention
to become a United States citizen.
By 1942, she had shortened her last name to Wills.
Author's Collection

William Howard Gaskell, Bad Sailor and Alabama Scofflaw

Bill was a different story all together. He was evolving into a real piece of work. Gaskell had just turned 12 when the war began in 1939. He was 14 when patriotic fervor swept the nation on December 8th, 1941, the day after the Japanese attack on Pearl Harbor. The nation huddled around their AM radios as President Roosevelt made his "...*a day that will live in infamy*" speech. Congress declares war on Japan. The naval base in Hawaii was in flames while America's men and women, young and old, wanted a piece of Japanese Emperor Hirohito and his West Pacific war machine. A military draft was almost unnecessary. Men were lined up for blocks at recruiting stations.

Bill Gaskell wanted in but was too young. One day he decided, "*I bet can fake my way into the military and then go kill some Gerries and Japs to help save the world for truth, justice and the American way and probably even get some free beer from the throngs of grateful civilians*".

Bill had a friend in the Hyde Park neighborhood. William Arthur Abbott lived at 5543 S Ingleside with his parents John and Nellie and older brother John Henry (Jack). Bill Abbott spent a lot of time hanging around with Bill Gaskell. Meanwhile, just a few hundred feet away, Enrico Fermi and his band of merry nuclear physicists were carefully assembling what would become the world's first self-sustaining nuclear reaction. This covert experiment was conducted under the west stands of U of C's Stagg Field right down the street at 56th and Ellis. Perhaps a radiation leak changed Billy G's brain chemistry just enough to influence his decision making over the next few years. One wonders.

One wonders how a man evolves into a trouble making scofflaw who graduates from youthful skullduggery into a multiple convicted felon. A man's path in this world usually finds its roots in his youth. Mother Agnes E. Gaskell gets some of the credit (blame?).

"Train up a child in the way he should go: and when he is old,
he will not depart from it" Proverbs 22:6 KJV

Bill left Hyde Park High School in his sophomore year. The balance of his education was at the street-level-high-school-of-hard-knocks. His father was not in the picture having relocated permanently to Oklahoma. Momma Gaskell was left to single-handedly corral him and his older brother Lawrence. The Gaskell boys were constantly getting into trouble with local law enforcement. So, mom hatched a plan to get young Bill into the United States armed forces ASAP. At least she would have one of her cantankerous kids off the street.

The military option creates an environment that has the potential to instill individuals with the personal direction and discipline beneficial to the common cause. Sixteen year old Billy "the Kid" Gaskell was a prime example of a young buck with the need for personal direction and discipline beneficial to the common cause. Momma Agnes could not have predicted that her youngest offspring would evolve into such a pain-in-the-ass to so many people close to him as well as to the societal collective that begged for the best out of individuals in those trying times. Of course, momma didn't want her youngest to be labeled a "slacker" either. Being an avid baseball fan, Bill may have thought, *"I'm gonna step up to the plate and hit a home run for the good old U.S. of A. and make my momma proud"*.

Mother and son began what I will call a convoluted process of getting Billy boy into the Navy. It started with Agnes pretending to be William Arthur Abbott's aunt and then fraudulently becoming his guardian. Bill paid Abbott 50 cents for his social Security card and Momma Agnes paid Abbott $5 to go along with the ruse.

According to Navy records, a claim was made to the Probate Court that Abbott's father was missing, his mom was dead and Agnes is his aunt. On November 12, 1943, Letters of Guardianship are issued by the Probate Court of the State of Illinois, sealed and witnessed by the clerk of the Probate Court of Cook County, Illinois. Agnes is now the proud aunt and legal guardian of her "nephew", William Arthur Abbott. A copy of that document was received by the Department of the Navy on November 13, 1943.

She then signs the official US government paperwork;

"CONSENT, DECLARATION OF PARENT OR GUARDIAN
in the enlistment of a minor under twenty-one years of age"

So, 16 year-old William Howard Gaskell, born January 12, 1927, entered the Navy as 17 year-old William Arthur Abbott, born in Chicago May 13, 1926. Gaskell made it official by using Abbott's birth certificate issued by the Chicago Board of Health. Bill Gaskell had "borrowed" the older Abbott's birth date, name and SSN. He got a head start on one of the plagues of our information age: identity theft.

Why didn't they just wait two months for Gaskell's 17th birthday on January 12, 1944? By then, the whole guardianship baloney and identity thievery would not have been necessary. I dunno. And where were Abbott's parents during all this? Apparently, they were kept out of the loop. Momma Agnes was desperate to get her Wayward William off the street pronto, ASAP and yesterday. Mission accomplished! Good job momma!

Bill's two-year tour of duty with the U.S. Navy began on November 27, 1943 at the Great Lakes Naval Training Station just north of Chicago. After completing basic training, he went home for a 2 week recruit leave and then to his first assignment in Gulfport, Mississippi. "William Arthur Abbott" reported for duty at the Armed Guard School on February 4, 1944.

16 year-old William Howard Gaskell, Chicago bad boy, masquerading as 17 year-old William Arthur Abbott, US Navy recruit.
Look out y'all, here comes trouble!
Author's Collection

The Navy Armed Guard was a little-known but critically important unit in the armed forces. US Navy sailors were assigned to merchant ships used to transfer troops, weapons, ammunition and other supplies. These merchant ships were mass-produced for the war effort in shipyards all around the gulf coast. Civilian Merchant Marines operated these "Liberty Ships". It was wartime and the Ships needed a little extra oomph to secure their cargo against enemy attack. They were fitted with anti-aircraft weapons such as 20mm cannons, 50 caliber machine guns and other defensive weaponry. Highly trained US Navy sailors, like our man of the hour, Bill Gaskell - I mean Abbott - operated these guns.

One of these ship building sites, the Wainwright Shipyard, was in Panama City, Florida. Bill's soon-to-be first wife was employed there as a food service worker in the civilian workforce. Hold that thought; we'll get back to that later.

Once Bill was trained to operate these anti-aircraft weapons in Gulfport, he transferred to the Armed Guard Center at the New Orleans Naval Base, on March 5, 1944. That recently decommissioned base is just across the Mississippi river from the Big Easy in Algiers, Louisiana. He received additional training there firing bigger guns at a target range further down the Mississippi at Shell Beach. Soon, he served his country on several of merchant ships including the S.S. CHOLUTECA, the S.S. REBECCA LUKENS and S.S. RICHARD K. CALL. During this time, the D-DAY invasion had occurred in France on June 6th 1944. His Navy unit stayed close to home providing cover for local munitions supply routes. This was still dangerous duty. German U-boats were known to patrol the United States east coast and Gulf of Mexico launching torpedoes at the merchant ships. Sadly, many ships and sailors went down in US waters victims of Deutschland's Navy subs.

Bill's final deployment was on the S.S. RICHARD K. CALL. This lasted from April 19, 1944 to July 8, 1944. That is when Bill really began to show his, shall we say, "playful" side. His mental cannon must have just become unhinged, beginning to roll freely on the deck of his young adventurous mind. This heralded the beginning of his slide into criminal behavior that would soon lead to felony convictions and prison time in the civilian world. *Aw shucks! He was just a little-old teenager having fun, right? C'mon now, boys will be boys.* Sorry, not during wartime. Bill would soon learn that military discipline trumps all. No sense of humor here. This last trip ended with him being transferred to the Armed Guard Center in Brooklyn, New York, for some well-deserved disciplinary action. On July 11, 1944, he was given 18 days restriction for the offense:

"Intoxicated ashore and disorderly conduct
on board the SS RICHARD K. CALL".

Everybody sing! *"What do you do with a drunken sailor?"* On August 17, 1944, Bill was transferred to the Naval Training Center, Newport, Rhode Island, for training and assignment to new construction ships. It appears that the wise and prudent Navy brass had second thoughts about him getting his naughty little hands on fully loaded, high-powered anti-aircraft weapons. Let's see how well he does with a paint brush balancing on 15 story tall scaffolding. Once safely tucked away in Newport, he soon completed training on the rifle range with a respectable score of 126, followed by fire fighter and water rescue schools.

Billy Boy requested and was granted a 2-week leave in late August of 1944. He told a little white lie by stating that he would be at home visiting his lonely momma at 5504 S. Kenwood in Chicago. He actually traveled to Panama City, Florida on September 7, to romance the young lass, Miss G (name deleted to protect her identity). She was that civilian food service worker at the Wainwright Shipyard he had met during his time at armed guard school. Bill attempted to scam the Navy claiming he had married during his leave. If successful, Miss G would soon begin receiving monthly allotment checks courtesy of Uncle Sam. This marriage did not happen as Bill stated and the monthly checks did not go out to "Mrs. Abbott". We'll clear that up later. Read on.

This guy was starting to look like a dude from "Central Casting". He got the usual manly-man tattoos of the day: "Death Before Dishonor" and a heart with "Mother" in the scroll. His heart was apparently in the right place but his head was somewhere else. His loose cannon was getting looser and looserer (sic).

By the end of September, 1944, he was habitually late for muster, got into frequent fights and started drinking to excess. Somehow, he managed to keep his balance on that 15 story tall scaffolding, paint brush in one hand and a beer bottle in the other. It sounds as if the heavy weight of adult responsibility was getting to this now 17 year-old. After missing two class periods, he was introduced to one of law enforcement's more effective tools created to instill discipline and steer the wayward ship of a man's conscience into the straight and narrow fjords of conformity: solitary confinement. Yessiree! A few nights in the "box" should get this little smart ass pointed in the right direction.

Two days on bread and water in the darkness of a six-by-eight room apparently had the opposite effect. It deepened Bill's resolve to buck the system and get back at "them bogus sumbitches". He was right and the world was all wrong.

Whatever patriotic visions he had back in November 1943, were dashed to bits upon the jagged rocky reefs of reality by late summer 1944. Things began to unravel quickly. Wild Bill stole a watch from a fellow sailor. While on duty the next day, he was carrying a concealed deadly weapon (i.e., a loaded revolver) and a blackjack. To top it off, he was topped off with several beers. That pretty much sealed the deal for this guy. The Navy was really pissed off now: underage drinking, drunk on duty and hiding a loaded stolen pistol. Uncle Sam winced and wisely commanded the commanders to take immediate corrective action. Game over, Billy.

His summary court martial convened and quickly reached a verdict on November 17, 1944: guilty by plea agreement on all charges. This convinced the wise and prudent Navy brass that they should now go their separate ways.

You would think that the armed forces would try to keep their enrollment up during wartime. He really did make an impression on the powers- that-be. It was clear to all that the impression made by this 17-year-old was not a good one. *You make your own bed and get to sleep in it* (sorry for all the clichés, but, *if the shoe fits.....*).

So, two days short of one year of service, November 25, 1944, Bill Abbott was awarded a Bad Conduct Discharge, as in "unfit for military service", the good old BCD. The Navy had enough cannons already and did not need any loose ones rattling around on the decks of warships during an actual war with actual lives on the line.

He voluntarily waived transportation from the Naval Training Center, Newport, Rhode Island, to the station nearest his home. Instead of finding his way back to Chicago, he traveled to the panhandle of Florida to marry his waiting fiancée. She was still employed at the Wainwright Shipyard cafeteria in Panama City. On December 2, 1944, Bill and Miss G were granted a marriage license and officially married. Their wedded bliss would soon be interrupted.

Miss G was born in Alabama just after World War One. She was part of a large farming family. Her parents and siblings moved to the panhandle of Florida, sometime after 1930 to continue farming. This must have been a rough life. Farming is tough anytime, but in the sweltering Deep South and during the depression, it must have been especially grueling. Farm families were known for having many children. A large census of little Future Farmers of America running around made for a built-in work force.

With the start of the War, her family had seen opportunities to get off the farm and do their part in defeating the Axis of Evil power trio, led by Germany's Der Fuhrer, with guest stars Japan's Emperor Hirohito and Italia's El Duce Mussolini. Miss G shared in the war effort by finding a civilian job at the shipyard. There she met that young sailor from Chicago.

Now that they were officially hitched, the young couple set up housekeeping in Panama City. Maybe life would be nice for a small town girl wedded to a charming young Navy veteran from the big city. Well, maybe not this time.

Vets were like rock stars during that war and I'm sure Bill impressed the young lady. He was a handsome, dashing young stud, awash in impetuous self-confidence and possessing a relentless youthful swagger. One wonders if he ever told Miss G the reason for his early discharge.

Wainwright shipyard civilian workers during the war.
One could speculate that Miss G is in this picture.
Courtesy of Bay County Florida Digital Photo Archive

Soft Targets, Easy Money

Back in Chicago, the December snow and freezing rain was in sharp contrast to the balmy Gulf Coast during the 1944 Christmas holidays. Bill informs momma Agnes that *"You can keep your 'white Christmas'. I'm staying here."*

He had just turned 18. His anti-aircraft weapon skills had no real parallel in the civilian world. *"What shall I do with the rest of my life?"*

No problem here – resourceful Bill became self-employed. Great idea! He started his own cash business. Let's call it *Billy Abbott's CIF Enterprises* (CIF as in Cash-In-Fist).

He opted to use breezy Panama City as the home base for a fledgling interstate venture. The Ex-Navy man made regular trips 180 miles west to ply his new trade in Mobile, Alabama. He would return from his business trips with fistfuls of cash which impressed his young bride. So how did he earn all this cash money brought back home to his lovely bride? *"Hey Bill, you got some splainin' to do."*

Curious Miss G says *"Hey, honey bunch. Did you get jobs painting houses for little old ladies? Fixing their cars? Helping the sweet Southern ladies of Mobile cross the street for tips?"* As it turns out, he *was* helping those sweet Southern ladies of Mobile. Bill was relieving those nice ladies of the heavy load of cash in their handbags. He was very persuasive insisting at gunpoint that they lighten their purses and hand over the contents to him. Cash-stations-on-the-hoof you could say. Cha-ching!

He found many of these cash-laden-ladies along the fashionable upscale Government Street. Back in the day, the locals called it "Millionaires Row". He found the right place to get the cash and make the dash back to Miss G – soft targets and easy money. There is some evidence that he used stolen cars for his transportation, ditching them before he could be tracked down and captured.

This Alabama gravy train soon ran out of steam. Local authorities were catching on to his tactics. On one of his 'Bama trips, he was ID'd as the assailant in five armed robberies. Wild Bill was arrested, jailed and charged. On April 25, 1945, he stood trial at the Rudolph Benz-designed Mobile County Alabama Courthouse. There he was convicted of armed robbery in two of the five heists in Mobile.

In the span of five short months, this 18-year-old man, possessing much intelligence and positive potential, is transformed from Navy enlisted man, fighting for right and freedom, into a convicted felon facing 20 years imprisonment. He chooses the turn onto life's dream shattered highway.

Naturally, he always professed his innocence, insisting that he was a northerner unjustly singled out in the deep South; just a damned Yankee varmint to them-thar locals, living proof that those Yankee devils should keep their wayward ways way north of the Mason-Dixon line. *"Y'all come down here and yooz gawna git what's comin' to ya, lemme tell ya boy."*

Meanwhile, back in Panama City, a wife sits waiting for the husband to return. Where the hell was he? Finally, she heard the news that her Navy hero hubby would be watched over and cared for by the Alabama Department of Corrections. Sheesh!

After sentencing, Bill was given classification hearings comprised of a series of tests and interviews designed to determine the best placement for him in the prison system. In his psychometric tests, he scored "Superior", which, on its own, sounds impressive; a positive trait to be aware of (or wary of) in this young felon. But, in the opinion of the astute director of classifications, a Mr. Atrey, Abbott was *completely devoid of moral and ethical standards*". The director came to this conclusion based upon this 18 year-old's confession and testimony in open court. So, combining his test results with his belligerent attitude and raucous emotional outbursts while in the Mobile jail, he was deemed a problematic inmate. There was only one place for a rascal like this: MAXIMUM SECURITY at Draper State prison.

Draper was constructed in 1939 with a capacity for 600 first-time male felony offenders. Located in Elmore County, Alabama, on State Highway 143, the facility replaced the Speigner Reformatory. Prisoners were housed in seven dormitory-style cellblocks, which included a segregation unit for the "problem" children.

This was not your average lock-em-up-and-throw-away-the-key kind of prison. Draper's stated goal was to maintain an appropriate level of security to eliminate escapes presenting no threats to the community, while at the same time providing adequate housing, education and productive work for the inmates. Considered innovative, it included vocational classes equipped to teach trades and crafts. Each inmate had an assigned job within the institution, either on a large farming operation, a furniture plant, or a vehicle garage.

Radio stations in the area played the Country-Western hits of the day. Prisoners tapped their feet, sharpened their shivs and brawled in the prison yard to early 1940's classics such as "Pistol Packin' Mama" (Al Dexter), the World War II song "Smoke On The Water" (Red Foley), "I'm Wasting My Tears On You" (Tex Ritter), "She Broke My Heart in Three Places" (Hoosier Hot Shots) and "Yesterdays Tears" (Ernest Tubbs). Luckily, Chicago Bill was a big fan of country music.

Sentenced to two consecutive 10-year terms in the Alabama penal system, this Chicago Yankee hoodlum 10th grade dropout was not welcomed with open arms by his fellow felons and the powers-that-be. Southern pride runs deep. In the 1940's, there was still plenty of that around in Jim Crow Alabama. Here we have an 18 year-old northerner jailed in the Deep South - not much in common with the general prison population - and they weren't gonna let him forget it by-golly-dad-gummit! Bill was totally out of his element (1) being a Yankee and (2) being a tough-guy wise-ass from Chicago. Predictably, that 1-2 punch led him to being involved in a long series of 1-2 punch infused jail yard brawls. According to Bill himself, he was pressured into these fights primarily due to this "Yankee-ism". The prison guards usually looked the other way, getting a kick out of the kick-ass carnage.

On two occasions, Bill opened up a fresh can of late autumn whoop-ass on a chap named J.E. Harris. The result of the brawl on November 11, 1951, was Mr. Harris needing a new set of teeth. Knuckle meets tooth. Knuckle wins. Surprisingly, no punishment was handed out for this. Maybe the beating was justified in the eyes of the guards. Perhaps Bill was only being his casual, adventurous, "kiss-my-ass-you-Johnny-reb-son-of-a-bitch" self? Perhaps Harris was making gay advances toward Bill. Maybe the guards were placing wagers on the outcome of the latest Pop! Bang! Boom! Knowing Bill, he was just demonstrating the "Chicago way" - a generous gesture on his part, taking time out from his busy prison schedule to expand the cultural horizons of a felon whose life experience probably never traveled north of the Mason-Dixon line.

"Up the river" was a term used to describe the disciplinary vacations awarded to prisoners for any breach of peace during their stay at this institution of restitution. Just like in the Navy, these "time-outs" were spent in solitary confinement. Wild Bill spent so much time up the river that he earned the nickname *Steamboat*. That alias became a tattoo on his upper right arm. Steamboat attempted an escape from prison on Jan 24, 1947. This got him ten lashes on his bare back in addition to a trip upstream. On another occasion, he earned two days on bread and water for possessing a miniature bottle of whiskey. How did he get whiskey while in maximum security? Did he win a bet with a prison guard for a deftly delivered demonstration of the "Chicago Way" to a culturally deprived derelict from the land of Dixie?

Bill lost half of his right index finger during his prison term. According to the records, he was on a detail working as a cloth inspector in the Alabama Cotton Mill in Speigner. On October 18, 1946, Bill grabbed a large wooden block used to turn rolls of cotton cloth. He then allegedly slipped causing the heavy wooden block to crush his finger. Years later after prison, he confessed to one of his wives that he conjured up the idea of smashing his finger to get medical leave from the cotton mill. I'm guessing he mangled that index digit more than he wanted to. Bill claimed the prison doctor performed the amputation without anesthetic. Why would they do such a thing to a nice polite Yankee boy? Mission accomplished - he got his time off. Then, resourceful as ever, he made a claim against the prison for his 'accident' and was awarded $225. That's a lotta dough in 1946.

Somehow, Bill mustered up some discipline. "Mr. Abbott-Gaskell" settled down and practiced a form of good behavior which pleased the parole Gods. This period of going-along-with-the-program led to his parole on May 14, 1952. After serving seven years of the 20-year sentence, he packed up his Chicago swagger, collected his $225 "finger money", gave them "the finger" and went home to live with Momma Agnes at 5504 S. Kenwood in Hyde Park. There, he would soon resume his criminal career using his real name, William Howard Gaskell.

_____ Prison

_____ Alabama

DISCIPILINARY BOARD

Date : June 1, 1951

Name of prisoner : William A. Abbott NN   Ser. No. 50746

Offense : Violating Department Rule # 7

The above named inmate admitted having in his possession (1) Small Miniature bottle of whiskey which Guard at back-gate found on his person.

Reported by : _____   Date : June 1, 1951

Action Placed in Solitary Confinement for a period of 48 hours on bread and water.

Bill went in front of the Disciplinary Board on June 1, 1951
for violating the department rule #7.
"The above named inmate admitted to having in his possession (1) small miniature bottle of whiskey which the guard at back gate found on his person. Placed in solitary confinement for a period of 48 hours on bread and water."
Author's Collection

I often wonder what happened to the original William Arthur Abbott. He probably changed his name and moved to the remote reaches of northern Idaho if he ever found out how his buddy Gaskell crapped all over his reputation. Or maybe he just opened up his own fresh can of whoop-ass on the young parolee.

According to the 1930 census in Illinois,, when the real William Abbott was four years old, he was housed at a Catholic institution called the Home for the Friendless, associated with the Christian Home Mission of Peoria, Illinois. Ten years later, he was living with his parents and brother Jack, a block away from the Gaskells in Chicago. After that, Abbott seems to have vanished. One could speculate that Abbott was

59

mentally challenged which could explain why he was housed at the Home in Peoria. Could that have been why he went along with momma Agnes on the identity deal? Perhaps John and Nellie fell upon hard times and needed to have William kept in a safe place for a while. No offense to any Abbotts out there but this is a little mystery I would like to solve. Do you know what happened to William Arthur Abbott, born May 13, 1926?

Oh, and what about Bill's spouse back in Florida? To her credit, she stuck by Bill and did the faithful wife thing. She traveled to visit Bill several times while he was in the Alabama-slammer. At some point, she was granted a divorce from husband-of-the-year, Mr. Chicago Felon and then married a nice fellow in the US Air Force. This union worked out much better for her. Those Air Force guys are known for their brain power, integrity and for flying under the radar. Congratulations on the happy ending!

A Liberty Ship built at the Wainwright Shipyard. Hundreds of ships of this design were mass produced for the war effort. Notice the anti-aircraft gun mounted on the stern.
Courtesy of Bay County Florida Digital Photo Archive

"….…..fighting-the-gag-reflex"

     I was 6 months old in December, 1950. We moved from the "Misery Mansion" two blocks away into the corner house at 5400 S. Ridgewood Court. The family was elated. Good job Dad! Built around 1890, the white stucco-wrapped structure was one of the largest single-family homes on the block. It had a second floor sun porch, white picket fence, several large shady trees available for climbing, four 2nd floor bedrooms and one very busy bathroom.

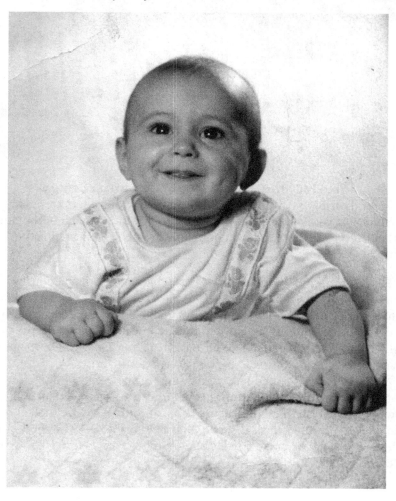

I was very, very happy with the new house.
Author's Collection

The shady front yard at 5400 S. Ridgewood Court.
Family friend, Alice Boarman, is watching youngsters frolic in
the grass. If you look closely, a boy is perched on a branch of the tree.
That tree is still there today although the house disappeared in 1961.
Author's Collection

A beautiful purple lilac bush bloomed conspicuously and vigorously in the corner of the yard along 54th Street. The base of that bush became the final resting place for our beloved departed pets over the next decade. Gold fish, hamsters, white mice and parakeets provided nourishment for that voracious old bush teaching us all the critical and inevitable lessons of the cycle of life. Viva la fertilizer!

This house seemed like a cavernous estate when compared to the 3-room apartment at the Dorchester mansion. It was a great house to grow up in. My earliest life memory is of sitting at the kitchen table watching my mother wash dishes while belting out 1940's show tunes with her eyes closed and a joyous smile on her face. Now I know why the caged bird sings.

Skeeter Boarman's sister fondles my favorite tree trunk.
Author's Collection

When you walked down the creaky wooden basement stairs, the aromatic intensity of coal hit you right away. Take a left turn at the bottom of the stairs and the coal bin was at your right, a bare light bulb stared you in the eye and the coal fired furnace sat menacingly on your left. That "octopus" furnace dominated the basement.

I remember the coal deliveries by a big old guy with a wheel barrow. He deftly poured the coal down a chute on the 54th Street side of the house. Those black chunks of dormant primeval energy formed a pile high in the NE corner of the basement. To the adults, the basement must have been a big smelly mess. I was fascinated by it but, at the same time, a bit wary of that poorly lit cobweb infested space with its stonewall foundation and a hint of mustiness in the air. Spooky! Someone mentioned that the "boogey man" was down there. Thanks a lot for telling me that. I already had enough nightmare material after seeing the 1935 movie "The Mummy" on TV's Shock Theater.

The collie stands watch over the yard near
the aforementioned lilac bush. Passersby were greeted
with a bombardment of barking from that pretty dog.
Author's collection

A white wringer washer, a stone utility sink, and a rusted white metal shower stall were at the west end of the basement with another single light bulb hanging from the ceiling. A wooden workbench stretched the length between two windows on the north wall. Dad kept his prized hand-made wooden toolbox there. A doorway led out the back to a storage space underneath the back porch. From there we could go to the backyard where Ma would hang clothes to dry. In later years, the backyard would serve as a parking space for my brother's cooler-than-cool black-and-white 1956 Ford Victoria.

There was a baby grand piano in the living room. My oldest sister Nancy was the main tickler of the 88s. She did a fine rendition of the "Hungarian Rhapsody No. 9". On the Saturday morning cartoons, Bugs Bunny also played that Rhapsody very well, and probably better. I still wanna be like Bugs Bunny. He was *my* childhood hero.

The most prominent feature of the room was the built-in floor-to-ceiling mirror with oak wood columns and framing, an impressive piece of workmanship. There was a small gap between it and the wall where I would secretly dump food that tasted bad to me (like yucky cole slaw and anything my father would flavor with wheat germ or dulce powder). I was either feeding mice or poisoning them.

That room is where the annual Christmas tree dominated the scene. Ah yes, the tinsel, shiny glass globe ornaments, the warm glow of the lights, nativity scene and the bright star on top. I couldn't figure out how Santa made it down our chimney since it went straight to the coal furnace in the basement, but I still believed in the cotton faced fellow. The chimney thing was his problem to solve.

Nancy had two serious accidents during her youth. Back in the misery mansion days, the 10-year old slipped on ice while carrying home a glass gallon of milk. Ice was in the lobby of the mansion due to a ceiling leak. Nancy's right hand received a very deep cut from the broken glass requiring many stitches courtesy of the Illinois Central Hospital on Stony Island Avenue. A lawsuit gave Nancy a nest egg to draw from for college. Then, in the summer of '53, the 14-year-old was knocked to the ground by a speeding car. This happened on 54th street right next to the house. I heard the commotion and ran over to investigate. A girl was lying on the ground. At first, I did not realize it was Nancy. When ma came out and started shrieking, it became apparent who it was. A broken arm, a cast and another lawsuit soon followed. A tough way to pay for college.

The Museum of Science and Industry as well as the 57th Street beach were a short one-mile walk from the house. Our visits there were always an exciting journey for me. Walk east on 56th Street underneath the Illinois Central train tracks, to Jackson Park, take a few minutes to test out the swings, the slide and the nausea-inducing merry-go-round and off we go to the beach.

We had the usual assortment of pets. Over the years, there were three collie dogs, Lady, Lassie and Laddie. We had them all but not at the same time. I remember Lassie the most.

Rumor has it that father was not happy with these dogs. According to one of my sisters, Wally took Laddie for a walk-of-no-return. Somehow he made Laddie disappear *and* he probably had a hand in the demise of Lassie in 1961. We'll save that discussion for later.

Then there was the furry black cat, Spitfire. Shortly after we moved into the house, one of my sisters found the kitten soaked in gasoline in the neighbor's yard. Someone in the 'hood was not a cat lover. After a bath and some tuna, that yellow-eyed cat stayed with us for at least ten years. Spitfire had a damaged left ear, maybe from the gasoline. Goldfish, hamsters, white mice and parakeets rounded out the family zoo.

Mid-summer family wackiness at the 57ᵗʰ Street beach.
Aunt Stella gets a good laugh from the antics of those crazy kids.
Author's Collection

We found a young blue jay in the front yard with a damaged wing. The girls of the house nursed it back to health. It flew away when it was able, but that blue jay would often come back and land on the front porch for a visit. Since then, jays have been my favorite wild bird. I love the beautiful mix of blue colored feathers. They have a nasty reputation for being discourteous to other feathered creatures but they sure are pretty.

There must have been a sale on light green interior wall paint. It was in just about every room. So, life was fine for six kids in a big new place to live. For us, this was a real mansion compared to the misery one. By this time, ma had decided that six was enough. She had completed her mission. Shortly after I was born, she had her "tubes tied".

This furry black kitty, Spitfire, kept me warm at night
with her body heat and massage-like purring.
Author's Collection

Laddie, Larry and an ice cream cone, 1953.
Those were my favorite pants despite the holes in the knees.
I liked them so much that I would pull them out from the pile
of smelly dirty laundry just so I could wear them one more time.
Funny the things you remember.
Author's Collection

Little did we know, Ma was just about to leave the family for her
great adventure when this picture was taken, summer 1953.
Little Larry (me) pets the big collie dog.
Author's Collection

Along with the new house came the growing chasm between Flo
and Wally. New responsibilities like mortgage, taxes, utility bills and
upkeep of the house fueled their discord. So maybe they could sit down
and discuss these new issues with compassion and the spirit of
compromise. Well, *that* didn't happen! Ma and Pa would have frequent
arguments - bouts of shouts – peppered with colorful name-calling. Some
of my favorites include *"You dumbbell you"*, *"Bitch"*, *"Son of a Bitch"*,
"Dumb cluck" and *"You don't have the brains God gave a goose"*. Ma
would often preface an argument with the phrase *"Say, listen you..."*.

In spite of all that, dad consumed himself with controlling every
aspect of what went on in the house. He made us run out and fetch the
Chicago Sun Times in the trash baskets on 53rd Street. When he came
home from work on cooler days, his first action upon entering the house
was to lower the thermostat without any discussion about if we were
comfortable. Washing dishes with hot water was a big no-no. Leave a
light on and you were on the receiving end of a high-decibel scolding.
Things like that, along with his fanaticism about eating the 'right foods',
help stoke the domestic nuclear chain reaction that led to the reason this
book exists.

I'm hamming it up at the 57th Street beach.
Author's Collection

Dad spent a lot of time shopping at the legendary Maxwell Street market. It was a crowded, busy street bazaar just south of downtown Chicago with open-air sidewalk vendors and shops selling shoes, nuts, candy, clothing, tools, sox, underwear, stuff that "fell off a truck" - everything a bargain hunter could ever want. The mouth-watering aroma of grilled onions and southern BBQ filled the air. One of dad's favorites was the raw nuts - peanuts, almonds, pecans, walnuts. We ate nuts. Lot's of nuts. The nutcracker was fun to use. It had an Archimedes screw handle that you twisted until the nutshell exploded with a sudden "crunch". Walnuts were especially explosive. Wear eye protection.

Dad would often bring home food that only he would eat because nobody else in the house would – avocados, cans of sockeye salmon and other fishy delights. I steered clear of him when he showed up with that weird stuff. I was becoming an expert in "avoidance behavior".

One benefit if his job as shipping clerk at Health Food Jobbers was that he could bring home damaged items returned from customers. There were dented cans of honey, vegetables, soybeans, and boxes of perfectly good dry cereal slashed open by a careless dockworker. Wally was on a first name basis with many vendors at the hectic Randolph Street markets. There he could buy his produce in bulk and then share a seat on the bus with a 50-pound bag of carrots. Wally was trying to be frugal by purchasing large quantities of raw fruits and vegetables. It was more like a "penny-wise-and-dollar-foolish" situation when a bushel of avocados became a 4/5 bushel of rotten avocados because nobody ate them but him. Decaying produce added that unique bouquet to the air in the house.

Then there was the sound of the vegetable grinder - Wally's weapon of machine mastication. I still have that thing and it works great. That, along with the hydraulic press, was his juice factory. Wally used a wooden plunger to force carrots, celery, green peppers, and assorted greens to surrender to the power of the 1800-RPM grinding wheel. Dad then wrapped the dripping pulp in cheesecloth and placed it into a square stainless steel pan with a drainage spout. Position the pan into the hydraulic press, tighten the relief valve screw, pump away and the juice flowed down the spout into a waiting cup. The color of the juice would be orange, or green, or mud depending upon what mix of vegetables and secret additives he was experimenting with on any particular day.

Dad's juice factory; the grinder on the left and the
hydraulic press at right. Today, the familiar grating noise
of the grinder sends me on an instant flashback to the 1950's.
Author's Collection

71

Plain carrot juice is tasty and sweet. I actually like it. Most of us did - even ma - but, dad would start mixing in whatever his latest fad additive was - brewers yeast, ground sunflower seeds, dulce and the dreaded cod liver oil. The vegetable juice mixtures were somewhat palatable if vegetables were the only ingredients. However, after Wally shoveled in the *really* "healthy" stuff, the juice could become absolutely, downright incomprehensibly frighteningly bad tasting. The phrase "fighting-the-gag-reflex" comes to mind. Then there was the classic "burping-up-of-cod-liver-oil", the real character builder. Ground-up sunflower seeds added to the juices made me choke. We were expected to partake of these 'treats' on a daily basis. "Just ignore the taste" dad would say. Could anyone envision a grinning three-year-old boy exuberantly holding out his cup and asking for a refill of Wally's strange brews? Mmmmmmaybe not.

Some of those volatile experiments were disposed of behind the aforementioned mirror in the front room. Otherwise, we had to force feed ourselves in view of Wally's menacing glare or buy time until we had to make a potty call. Well, you know, a prisoner of war has to be creative in search of the appropriate survival technique. What does one do with weird sickly-green vegetable juice with dulce blended with wheat germ flakes, brewer's yeast and cod liver oil? I wonder how those flushed concoctions complicated the wastewater treatment process in Chicago.

On the other hand, Ma Flo was a kinder, gentler keeper of treats. She made chocolate chip cookies with walnuts. Enough said? Flo often cajoled Wally into making regular trips to the 53rd street Walgreen's drug store to bring home pints of their great ice cream. I would volunteer to make the trip so they would not forget the Fudge Ripple and Ma's New York Cherry. In the 1950's, Walgreen's had some alluring TV commercials about their ice cream. Watching them made me feel cooler.

We were not an "ethnic" Polish family. With Flo and her sisters being raised in a boarding school, Polish language and customs did not become part of their lives and consequently not ours. We rarely had any Polish food. That was limited to old-fashioned kielbasa at a wedding reception, and maybe a pierogi here and there sent home from Gramma Sofie. The closest we came to the Polish language was either dad cussing out Flo or eavesdropping on phone calls between dad, his siblings and "busha", Gramma Sofie. Sofie would give Wally snacks to bring home to us but they rarely made it into the house. He would toss those homemade baked goods into the trash on his way home. I suspect he would sneak a nibble or two on those freshly baked cheese, apricot and poppy seed kolacz before discarding them. After performing this quality control, Wally decided that pastries were not quite appropriate for family consumption. Such a noble and responsible act could have qualified Walter to be in the running for Father-Of-The-Year. What a guy!

William Howard Gaskell Comes Home

In May 1952, 25-year-old William Howard Gaskell began his parole from the Alabama prison system after serving seven years of a twenty-year sentence as William Arthur Abbott. Now he could relax, look for a job and just be Bill Gaskell again. The job skills learned while a guest of the Alabama DOC included Methods Of Pointing A Gun At Victims (MOPAGAV), Advanced Armed Robbery Techniques (AART), Prison Escape for Beginners (PEB) and Basics of Surviving Solitary Confinement for Wise-Ass Yankee Caucasians (BSSCWAYC). These skills would once again come in handy for the young lad.

He went home to stay with his mother. Her Kenwood Avenue apartment was just two short blocks from our house. In a valiant effort to travel the straight-and-narrow as a hard working ex-con, he landed a job as a laborer at the US Steel South Works. This was a sprawling 80-acre complex on the shore of Lake Michigan at 87th Street. He traveled that road for a while, but a longer, more exciting road was his destiny. I tried to get information from US Steel about him but they denied my request. Apparently, they do not perform genealogical searches for the general public. Where is that subpoena when I need it?

Shortly after returning from prison, Bill met a married woman. Exactly how Flo and Bill met is unclear. One theory is that they met through my Aunt Stella, ma's older sister. While sorting out Stella's personal effects after her death in 2006, I found a hand-written resume' of hers. That document revealed that she held a job at the US Steel South Works before her 1955 move to Kalamazoo, Michigan. Stella also may have lived in the same apartment building as Gaskell for a time. So, it is probable that Stella and Bill knew each other both at work and in the neighborhood.

Stella was single, never married, two years older than Flo. Maybe Bill tried to date Stella. I can envision a scenario where Bill asked Stella to meet him for a beer at a local establishment. Stella asks sister Flo to accompany her to chaperone the meeting that day. Flo meets Bill.

Ma once told me there were taverns in the area she would frequent with Stella. They liked to share a beer from time to time and listen to the latest music on the juke box. Lake Park Avenue was home to many of those watering holes. One still open today is Jimmy's Woodlawn Tap at 55th and Woodlawn. It survived the great urban renewal of the fifties and sixties and a push by the locals in later years to close it down. It has been a favorite spot for the University of Chicago crowd since it opened in the 1940's. It is located four blocks from our corner house and two blocks from where Gaskell lived with his mom at the time.

East 55th Street in the 1940's. Locals called this bustling area of small shops and taverns "The Gulch". At this time, Agnes Gaskell lived nearby waiting for her son to return home from the Alabama prison. Every building you see in this picture was demolished in the 1950's and 60's for the University of Chicago urban renewal project.

Courtesy Special Collections Research Center, University of Chicago Library

There is a common misconception about the cultural make-up of the Hyde Park neighborhood especially now since a real live President of the United States resides there. Recall that Hyde Park was the site of the Columbian Exposition of 1893. Jackson Park and the Museum of Science and Industry are remnants of that event. There still are some historic and lavish mansions in the area. Many of the intelligentsia from the University of Chicago resided there along with business and political leaders.

Our house was in the area known as "Hyde Park Center". This is the oldest section of Hyde Park and was home mainly to the working class. Much of this early housing stock was home to the laborers who built and worked for the exposition. It was a mix of modest brick or frame single family homes along with apartment buildings dating back to the building boom of the 1880's and 1890's. Many mixed-use multistory buildings, taverns, deli's and restaurants lined the main streets of 53rd, 55th, Cottage Grove, Stony Island and Lake Park Avenue. Local businesses thrived during the decades since the exposition.

Then came urban renewal beginning in the 1950's. Large areas were cleared of the old buildings to make way for the U of C expansion and, ultimately to 'clean up' and modernize the area. In addition to the new cookie-cutter brick townhouses scattered about, the controversial University Apartments appeared in the middle of 55th Street. This tidal wave of demolition and new construction continued until civic groups protested that beautiful and historic structures - the character of old Hyde Park - would be lost forever. Some accused the city and university of racist motives for the renewal plans. Whatever the reasons, for better or for worse, the old Hyde Park we knew is mostly gone, drastically different now, modernized and gentrified beyond all recognition. Still a great place to live and probably better now that an ex-POTUS named Barack requires Secret Service surveillance 24/7.

Looking west on 55th Street at Lake Park about 1956
before urban renewal made most of these structures vanish.
The only building still standing today is the former Chevrolet
dealership on the left foreground. The Hyde Park Shopping Center
replaced the buildings and the corner tavern on the right.
Courtesy Special Collections Research Center, University of Chicago Library

75

So, how Bill and Flo met will always remain a mini-mystery. Wally and Bill could not have been more different. My dad was somewhat quiet, reserved and a hard working homebody trying to keep himself and his family healthy while stretching each dollar to its molecular level breaking point. He did not have any friends to speak of except for an old retired boxer with a cauliflower ear named Stanley Bisek. Stanley would visit once in a while but we didn't know much about him.

Then there was Bill, a gregarious spontaneous scofflaw party-animal who lived to smoke Lucky Strikes, drink Budweiser, dance until dawn and just plain old hang around. After surviving seven years imprisoned in the Land of Dixie, he was ready to roll up his t-shirt sleeves, light up a smoke and get down to the serious business of womanizing and partying. There's gonna be trouble in the neighborhood!

The Big Bang

When exactly did Flo and Bill take off for their great adventure? Here's a clue: Bill had to report to his parole officer downtown once a month starting in November 1952. Failure to report would compel the Alabama authorities to suspend parole and welcome the parolee back into custody. This circumstance would usually require the offender to complete his entire original sentence. A fugitive warrant for Bill's arrest was published, stating he had become delinquent as of December 3rd, 1953. Lucky for Bill the warrant was for Abbott, not Gaskell. He was not Abbott anymore but law enforcement did not have a clue *yet*. Abbott, for all intents and purposes, was now a ghost. Gaskell had no prison record or Navy Bad Conduct Discharge. He was just a good old boy out there having fun with a married mother of six – as free as a couple of love-birds could be.

Dad suspected that there was something going on. He grilled Flo from time to time triggering shouting matches that often started in the kitchen and concluded in the front yard. Ma would often go out and have a few beers. Wally ordered 10 year-old Loretta to follow Ma and report any details she could remember. The young girl was very nervous about this. She complained about being put in the middle of a suspected affair. On one occasion, Loretta followed Flo and Bill on a long walk through Jackson Park. She was sure that Ma saw her once but never confronted Loretta about it. The chasm between my parents was widening and eventually reached the breaking point.

Ma's adventure with Bill began in November, 1953. This was soon after Halloween and Bill's early November visit with his parole officer. Ma packed a suitcase for the trip. Then they hopped in a car and split for the great southwest along historic Route 66. That highway, often called "The Mother Road", had become the route of choice for folks traveling between Chicago and Los Angeles and all points in between. Motels, shops, gas stations and tourist attractions beckoned the war-weary Americans to hit the road and "See the USA in a Chevrolet" or "Leave the Driving to Us" on the Greyhound bus. The popularity of the Mother Road inspired a TV show and the classic song "Get Your Kicks on Route 66". These days there are tours, books, maps and clubs all dedicated to keeping the Route 66 dream alive. Signs proclaiming "Historic Route 66" can now be seen along the route from Chicago, through Berwyn and on to Los Angeles.

What car did they drive? Bill had been suspected of auto larceny more than once. A 1947 black Chevrolet was mentioned in the records. Let's just say they had wheels and they used them.

Imagine the excitement of driving around the United States in the early 1950s, seeing the USA in a stolen Chevrolet. Bill is cruising at 50 MPH flicking cigarette butts out the window trying to hit road signs – his version of a stupid human trick. Ma's dark brown hair is waving in the breeze while she spins the dial on the AM radio trying to find a song she can sing along with. Good times for Flo and Bill.

The backdrop to all this hot fun was the cold war with the USSR. The McCarthy era was in full swing with Communists lurking behind every bush infusing the Hollywood movie machine with their "Godless propaganda". The interstate highway system was still in the planning stage by the Eisenhower Administration. The middle class was on the rise as heroic Korean War veterans came home. Television was becoming a regular part of American life. Elvis was growing up in Tupelo Mississippi. Hit songs on the radio included Dean Martin's *That's Amore*, Patti Page barking out *How Much Is That Doggy In The Window*, Hank Williams planting a guilt trip with *Your Cheatin' Heart*, Bill Haley and His Comets jamming *Crazy Man, Crazy* and blue-eyed Frank Sinatra declaring *I've Got The World On A String*. Hit movies include *From Here To Eternity, War Of The Worlds, The House Of Wax, Stalag 17* and *The Big Heat*, some of them Oscar winners.

Did ma leave a farewell note? How did the six kids find out she had left? Maybe it was just quiet in the house for a change - the yelling finally stopped. Since Bill had few legitimate marketable skills and Flo was basically an accomplished housewife and six-time baby maker, the couple needed a way to finance their romance before it became a nuisance.

Flo And Bill's Cross-Country Tour

As a purely practical matter, the typical traveler needs spending money for the small things like food, gasoline, lodging and ammunition for a .25 caliber Colt debit card.

STATE DEPARTMENT
OF
CORRECTIONS AND INSTITUTIONS
MONTGOMERY 4, ALABAMA

Gaskell

FUGITIVE WARRANT

To ANY PEACE OFFICER

WHEREAS WILLIAM A. ABBOTT Serial Number 50149 was convicted of the crime of ROBBERY 2cd in the Circuit Court of Mobile County, Alabama, on to-wit: The 25 day of April 1945; that thereupon the said convict was sentenced to imprisonment in the Alabama State Penitentiary for a term of: 20 YEARS; that the said convict was thereupon confined in said penitentiary in accordance with said sentence; that thereafter and to-wit: On the 14 day of May 1952, the said convict was paroled by the State Board of Pardons and Paroles, pending good behavior: Then on the 1 day of December 1953, the State Board of Pardons and Paroles declared said parolee delinquent and ordered said parolee arrested and returned to the confines of the penitentiary to appear before the State Board of Pardons and Paroles who will determine the Parole Status of said parolee.

THEREFORE, the undersigned of the State Department of Corrections and Institutions by virtue of the authority conferred upon him by the State of Alabama, does hereby authorize and direct you to retake the said parole violator wherever he may be found, for his return to the said State Department of Corrections and Institutions, situated in Montgomery in the State of Alabama.

IN TESTIMONY THEREOF, I have hereunto set my

hand and the seal of the Department of Correc-

tions and Institutions this the 4 day of

JUNE 19 54.

J. M. McCullough, Jr.
D I R E C T O R
State Department of Corrections and Institutions

Form 1---Par Del

A nationwide fugitive arrest warrant was issued when
Bill missed the December, 1953, visit with his parole officer.
Notice that the warrant names Abbott. The bad boy had nothing
to worry about. This was just another law to ignore since he was
Gaskell now, not Abbott - definitely flying under the radar!
Author's Collection

The record shows they perfected a casual style of armed robbery. It allowed them to make withdrawals from a variety of cash registers from Chicago to California and then all the way back to Bill's former Florida stomping grounds. Bill was the experienced armed felon and front man with the muscle while Flo gleefully drove the getaway car. This "M. O." (Modus Operandi – a Latin phrase meaning method of operation) was reported by eyewitnesses and law enforcement all across this great land of ours.

Ma's younger sister Helen had her brush with Hollywood fame in 1941. Always the dreamer, Flo wanted some of that excitement in her life too. The felonious couple now had plenty of time to explore the studios and legendary haunts of the rich and famous. Florence wanted her picture taken with a movie star and even hoped to land an audition. However, that wasn't going to happen on this trip. After some cash withdrawals in Pasadena, they had to make tracks out of town. Florida was in their sights.

Some compare Flo and Bill's exploits to the most notorious outlaw couple in United States history, Bonnie and Clyde. B & C were not very nice. They were so not-very-nice that they were deadly. They killed civilians *and* police. Consequently, the outlaw career of B & C ended in a hail of gunfire on a rural Louisiana back road, a deserving legacy to a dangerous pair.

To their "credit", F & B only hurt the feelings of their victims – they never pulled the trigger. Bill's .25 caliber Colt pistol was used strictly as the weapon of mass intimidation. It was a show of force employed to get Bill's point across to his latest random, but ultimately, cooperative benefactor. The bandit was getting so proficient with the intimidation thing that he used a wrench for one of his thefts instead of the gun. Cool daddy-o! Slick-o-matic! My ma could have used the nickname "Cash Flo". Oh, and how about "Dollar Bill"? So now we have "The Adventures of Cash-Flo and Dollar-Bill". Alright, that's a stretch but not bad given the context.

They paid about 20 cents a gallon for gasoline back then. Cigarettes were 25 cents a pack. F & B enjoyed a cold Budweiser together from time to time, spending about 50 cents a quart. They had plenty of cash to support their lifestyle. *"Fill 'er up, check the oil and empty the cash register, OK buddy? Make it snappy or I'll plug ya!"*

The following list is representative of eyewitness accounts of the pair: a handsome dark haired pistol packing young man and a dark haired pretty woman driving the speeding getaway car. They made quite a haul. Adjusted for inflation, in seven months they bagged in the neighborhood of $90,000 in today's money. Life was comfortable for them.

The list of their dubious achievements spread around the country reads like a travel itinerary.

To wit:

Oak Park Illinois, Western Union, robbery, $200
Oklahoma city, Oklahoma, Western Union, robbery, $600
El Paso, Texas, restaurant, robbery, $150
Phoenix, Arizona, drug store, robbery, amount unknown
Pasadena, California, Western Union, robbery, $150
Pasadena, California, Safeway Super Mart, robbery, amount unknown
Pasadena, California, Super Mart, robbery, $200
Pasadena, California, Drug store, robbery, amount unknown
Pasadena, California, Restaurant, burglary, money and food
Miami, Florida, Restaurant, 3 burglaries, money and food
Miami, Florida, laundry, burglary, amount unknown
Miami, Florida, Kosher delicatessen, robbery, $70
Miami, Florida, used car lot, auto larceny, 1946 or 47 Chevrolet
Miami Beach, Florida, Western Union, robbery interrupted, fled
Miami Beach, Florida, vegetable market, robbery, amount unknown
Miami Beach, Florida, restaurant, robbery, cigars/cigarettes/candy
Panama City, Florida, theater, robbery, $1600
Pensacola, Florida, theater, robbery, $600
Sarasota, Florida, Morrison's cafeteria, robbery, $800
Sarasota, Florida, Plaza restaurant, robbery, $600
St Petersburg, Florida, restaurant, robbery, $200
St Petersburg, Florida, Western Union, robbery, $150
St Petersburg, Florida, gas station, robbery, $220
St Petersburg, Florida, restaurant, burglary, hams/bacon/cigarettes
Tallahassee, Florida, theater, robbery, $800 (bank moneybag)
Tallahassee, Florida, theater, robbery, $500
Tallahassee, Florida, restaurant, robbery, $300

At some point during their little spree, they obtained a black-over-cream 1951 Chevrolet possibly in New Orleans. Given Bill's sense of humor and spontaneous nature, and since they purchased the Chevy with their 'earnings', he may have considered getting a 100% rebate. This would have been easily accomplished by carefully pointing his .25 caliber persuader in the face of the auto salesman. Flo was a little more practical and levelheaded. She would have talked him out of it citing the obvious fact that the personal info on the car title would most likely be used to ID them.

About halfway through their seven-month vacation together, they pulled a few jobs in and around Tallahassee and Miami. On February 7th, 1954, they hit the Spanish Plaza restaurant in Sarasota.

Sarasota Herald-Tribune

United Press Service
Associated Press Service

SARASOTA, FLORIDA, MONDAY MORNING, FEBRUARY 8, 1954

Entered At Second Class Mat
Post Office At Sarasota, F

Bandit Holds Up City Restaurant

In a matter of second last night, an armed bandit held up a fashionable restaurant in downtown Sarasota and escaped with between $600 and $1,000 in cash.

About 9:10 p. m. a man described as being about 40 years old, five feet eight or 10 inches tall, walked into the Plaza Restaurant at 1426 First Street and asked the cashier, Mrs. Pauline Williams, to ,"give me change for a dollar." according to Randy Hagerman, manager of the establishment.

Pulls Short Pistol

While Mrs. Williams was making change for the dollar, the man pulled a short pistol from his pocket and demanded, "Give it to me," the manager related. He took all the bills in the cash register and left probably between $35 and $50 in change. Hagerman said.

The manager said that as he was walking out of the kitchen, about 30 feet from the front of the main dining room, the man entered the front door next to the cashier's stand.

As soon as he saw the bandit, Hagerman said he was suspicious of him. "Even if he had a sign on his back, it couldn't have been plainer that there was something out of place about him," he added. "He just looked like he didn't belong. He was rough looking."

Hagerman said that after he saw the man he started to walk directly to the cashier's stand. But so fast was the bandit that by the time Hagerman reached the front of the restaurant the hold up had already been pulled and the bandit was escaping out the front door. Hagerman said he followed the

(Continued on Page 2, Col. 8)

(Continued from Page 1)

man in time to see him getting away in an automobile which evidently had been parked directly in front of the restaurant. One of the waiters said he saw a woman at the wheel of the car.

Wore Slouch Hat

The bandit was dark complexioned, Hagerman related, heavy set and wore an old slouch hat. He seemed to be wearing a dark zipper windbreaker, he added. Another witness to the holdup further described the bandit as wearing glasses.

About 35 to 40 people were in the main dining room of the restaurant at the time of the holdup, Hagerman estimated. He said it happened so fast that no one screamed or got excited. After the man made his getaway, however, he said that Mrs. Williams was overcome with shock and became hysterical. She was taken home and police officers were unable to question her for some time.

The robbery came just four days after a bandit described as 55 or 60 years old, about five feet nine inches tall and weighing about 140 pounds held up the Gulf Loan Company, 57 South Pineapple Avenue, in mid-afternoon of about $180. Officers are still investigating that robbery.

Robbed 11 Months Ago

About 11 months ago the Plaza was robbed of about $4,200 by three armed bandits about 2 a. m. in the morning. The men entered through the back of the restaurant, tied up the night watchman and broke open the safe. That robbery is still being investigated and none of the money has been recovered.

Within two minutes after last night's robbery an area-wide search was underway for the bandit. The Sarasota County sheriff's office, Venice police, and the Florida Highway Patrol were aiding city police in hunting the thief.

Soon, cupid started shooting arrows aimed at the Bandit's raucous little heart. Bill admitted he was growing very fond of Flo and needed to demonstrate his blooming affection for this married mother of six. They were having so much fun traveling together that marriage became the next logical step. Why worry about details such as "Florence is still married to Walter" and stuff like that. Flo conveniently contradicts conventional morals and assumes the alias 'Florence Williams' for the marriage license. Next stop on the cross-country tour: Las Vegas, Nevada. Judge John Lytle seals the deal on March 3, 1954. Enter Mr. and Mrs. William Gaskell. Flo is now Bill's second wife.

Bill Gaskell snapped this pic of Flo and a four legged accomplice.
It looks like their Chevy getaway car is in the background.
I'm guessing this was in the mountains taken right around the time
they got hitched in Las Vegas. I'm not sure but is that creature
a donkey, burrow or just a plain old ass? After much thought and
deep contemplation, I am not sure who the ass was in this whole story.
Author's Collection

A week later, they traveled back to lovely Sarasota, to see the sights and continue their honeymoon. They must have enjoyed visiting the Ringling Brothers winter home there. The couple arrived just in time for the Boston Red Sox spring training games. Bill was a huge baseball fan with a photographic recall of batting averages, pitcher's stats and home run records. Actress Dorothy Lamoure was known as the "Bond Bombshell" for her efforts during WW2 selling War Bonds. She had just thrown out the ceremonial first pitch at the Payne Park Baseball Stadium. Play ball!

While in Sarasota, Flo decided she needed to purchase her own personal persuader. Maybe she was thinking of doing some side jobs when Bill was busy. Perhaps they were gonna switch roles; let Bill do the driving for a change. Let's entertain the theory that Flo could have felt a need for personal protection from bad boy Bill. He could be a bit gruff with her. So, on March 17th, 1954, Flo casually looked over the inventory at the Jules Surplus Store at 1745 Main Street. The proprietor, Mrs. Jules Lancer, helped her with a purchase. Flo took a liking to the brown-handled .25 caliber Colt pistol behind the counter. It was identical to Bill's. Now they had two guns to play with.

The world was their cash cow, their golden egg-laying goose, their pearl laden oyster, their personal ATM before anyone outside of MIT ever envisioned such a machine. In late May, 1954, they decided to lay low after a theater job in Tallahassee. Everyone needs a break. F & B take a few weeks off to count the money, refresh the soul, lay on the beach, sip some suds, buy some duds, and live the good life or some version of that.

The freewheeling lifestyle of these imprudent little lovebirds was nearing its inevitable finale. I know what you are thinking. The coppers were finally going to catch up with them, surround them with spotlights, German Shepherd attack dogs, drawn pistols, with the officer-in-charge using his megaphone ordering them to *"Come out with your hands up!"* Officers then force F & B to lie face-down in the motel parking lot, slap on the bracelets and put an end to their road trip party. Well, that's not what happened. Let's just say that storm clouds were gathering for the pair, and I don't mean Florida's hurricane season. My Dad once told me something about Ma and I quote, *"She'll turn on you"*.

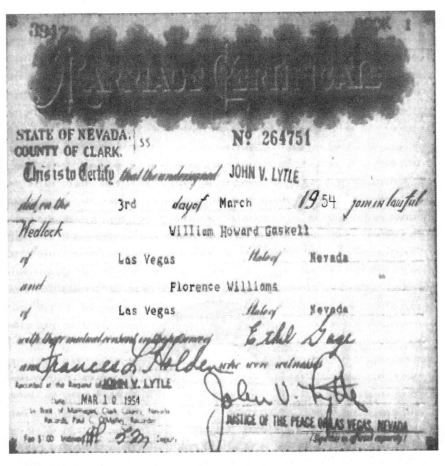

STATE OF NEVADA.
COUNTY OF CLARK. }ss

N? 264751

This is to Certify *that the undersigned* JOHN V. LYTLE

did on the 3rd *day of* March 19 54 *join in lawful*

Wedlock William Howard Gaskell

of Las Vegas *State of* Nevada

and Florence Williams

of Las Vegas *State of* Nevada

with their mutual consent in the presence of Ethel Gage

and Frances L. Holden who were witnesses

Executed at the Request of JOHN V. LYTLE

Date MAR 1 0 1954

In Book of Marriages, Clark County, Nevada
Records, Paul C. O'Malley, Recorder

Fee $1.00 Received

JUSTICE OF THE PEACE OF LAS VEGAS, NEVADA
(Signature or official capacity)

Florence "Williams" takes a gamble at life and marries
William Howard Gaskell in Las Vegas, March 3, 1954.
*"Hey ma, um, I know it's probably none of my business, but
... ain't you supposed to be divorced first?"*
Since she was already married, Flo needed to use
an alias to, as the certificate states, *"....join in lawful wedlock".*
Author's Collection

Flo smiling big for Bill's camera. She is in front of a structure
in an unknown part of the country. There is a plaque on the wall
that reads "WPA USA". That's a clue.
Author's Collection

Flo smiling for Bill's camera again. This time in front of the Water's Edge resort on the gulf coast near Panama City, Florida, 1954.
Author's Collection

News flash from south Florida; Something is just about to hit the fan.

THE BIG BANG IN MIAMI

"...she "spilled the beans" on him for reasons not made clear"

Dade County, Florida. June 7, 1954. Flo and Bill are hiding out in a Miami motel - laying low after their last "withdrawals" from two theaters and a Western Union in northern Florida. There were many motels in the area. They could have been at the Palms Motel or maybe the Sea Breeze Motel on Collins Avenue. I think my mother would have liked the name Sea Breeze. Also on Collins, there was the Carousel Apartment Motel and the Sahara Motel. The landmark Fontainebleau Hotel sounds like a great place to disappear in. It is conveniently situated in the heart of Miami's Millionaire's Row; a familiar nickname to Bill. The mention of another millionaire's row must have brought back lovely memories of those easy targets on Government Street in Alabama.

South Florida has long been the 'Land-to-Dispose-of-Your-Income' for vacationers from all over the globe. Visitors from England, France, Scandinavia and the Communist Bloc flocked to the Star-Spangled winter haven. Let's not forget the shivering masses from the north. Flocks of vacationers, known as "snow birds", made their annual migration from the frozen tundras of Wisconsin, Minnesota, Michigan and the lake-effect-snow regions of Indiana and New York.

Bill now had his eye on the riches of Dade County. Instead of laying low and sunning himself by the pool, Wacky William waywardly wandered the highways and back roads of the region to gather food, booze and his tobacco related fixations by any means necessary. He resorted to stealthy nocturnal burglaries and face-to-face bold-as-brass daylight robberies. Bill was compelled to ply his trade providing for his mate the best way he knew how.

Police records show that Bill had an acquaintance in the area. A fellow Alabama parolee lived in Miami. There he managed a typical gas station of the day. In those times, friendly uniformed attendants at your corner filling stations would gladly pump your gas, clean your windshield, check your tires and oil. Self-service refueling stops were unheard of. So, now Bill had a buddy to hang out with when he needed a time out from Flo.

For reasons known only to that hungry Palmetto bug crawling across the motel bathroom floor, the felonious couple had a major falling out. Flo was getting cranky again. Maybe Bill was spending too much time partying with his old friend. Maybe Bill's wise-cracking and beer drinking got to Flo. Possibly she had grown weary of the stimulating discussions about baseball batting averages, Budweiser versus Hamm's, Lucky Strikes versus Marlboros. Maybe it was the frustration over pointless petty disagreements like the correct pronunciation of the city of

Beaumont, Texas. They actually had that debate while driving east through Texas on highway US 90. Bill kicked Flo out of the car because she had won the pronunciation game – "Bo-mont vs. Bew-mont". But sweet Bill had second thoughts. He couldn't leave his faithful get-away driver stranded on a long hot dusty road. Adventurous gals like Flo Baran are hard to find. So, Bill turned the car around, fired up the charm and coaxed her back into the passenger seat where they kissed, made up and sped off to continue their adventure in Florida. Anyway, by now, the housewife was making plans for an exciting exit. It has been said that there are 50 ways to leave your lover. Flo gets credit for number 51.

Gas stations at the corner of US 1 and Lejuene Avenue, 1954
Courtesy Don Boyd

Perhaps Flo's mothering instincts kicked in and she began to pine for the white picket fence in Chicago, the adulation of the two sons and four daughters and the daily debates with her first mate about the merits of soy bean meal pancakes and dulce-infused whole wheat breakfast cereal as well as how best to conserve energy and water resources at their corner home. My 4th birthday was coming up in two weeks. Did she miss me? Maybe it was getting too damned hot down there. Or, dare I say, Boisterous Belligerent Bill was just becoming an Ardent Aggravating Arsehole!

Probably a mixture of all those little reasons prompted my Ma to call the Dade County Sheriff and report an armed parole violator from the Alabama prison system. She reported that the man was using an alias and hiding in a nearby motel. For good measure, Flo composed a note to the motel manager warning him of a gun-toting bad guy in one of his rooms. No worries. He should expect the Dade County Sheriff to arrive soon to take charge of the situation and restore law and order.

Flagler Street, downtown Miami, 1954. The picture shows Ma driving her black-over-cream Chevrolet right behind that white-over-black Cadillac. She was heading north on US 41. Destination – Chicago! (Hah! Hah! Gotcha!)
Courtesy Don Boyd

While Bill was in the shower, Ma did it. She hurriedly packed her suitcase with some of her clothes making sure to take her gun, a box of .25 caliber bullets and Bill's old work ID badge from Chicago's US Steel South Works. She fired up the 90 horsepower straight-six Chevy engine and hit the road bound for the Land of Lincoln. The snowbird left the shitbird before she became a jailbird.

It is interesting to note that highway US 41 starts in Miami on one end and terminates north of Chicago on the other end. Ma had an easy escape route. By simply following the US 41 signs north through sunny Florida, peachy Georgia, Nashville-y hilly Tennessee, blue-grass Kentucky and Hoosier Indiana, she would wind up on Chicago's Lake Shore Drive right at the Museum of Science and Industry in Jackson Park just four short blocks from home. She could leave the past behind, get some revenge on her boyfriend for some real or imagined transgression, ("She'll turn on you"), perform a valuable community service by getting a dangerous felon off the street and then resume her mercurial role as wife and mother. I imagine she may have even missed the carrot juice, brewer's yeast and steely stare of that grey-haired son-of-a-bitch husband of 16 years. Well, maybe not that last one.

When I was very young, ma told me a story of an accident she had while driving home from Florida. I thought it was interesting but it never occurred to me to ask the question *"What were you doing in Florida?"* Maybe I did ask but don't remember what she said. Somewhere during her escape from the sunshine state, she stopped to buy a dozen watermelons. She drove off with visions of her smiling children gnawing away on large crescents of bright red and green summer fruit. She imagines being back home and the past is fading memory. If I know my mother, she was singing songs to pass the time during her three-day drive. She had her favorites. Maybe it was the 1930's classic *Deep Purple* or Sinatra's *Chicago – that toddlin' town* or Judy Garland's *Somewhere over the Rainbow* melting her hardened heart when the song reminded of the movie phrase *"there's no place like home... there's no place like home.... there's no place ...."*. Stop day-dreaming Ma. You're driving a car.

As she was rounding a curve, the passenger-side tires left the road and the car started to skid on the gravel shoulder. She over-corrected to the left and the car suddenly caught traction sideways, rolled over once and landed back upright. Some of the watermelons smashed to bits, filling the car interior with a sticky-sweet crimson mess. By the Grace of God, and a whole lotta luck, she was not hurt. There was the dented car roof but no other damage appeared except some scratches in the paint. Not surprising as those cars from the fifties were made of real steel akin to armored personnel carriers. Ma had a quaint habit of collecting four leaf clovers over the years and they finally paid off! After forcing the roof back into shape, she continued on her journey. Just recently, that story came back to me along with the realization that the incident could only have occurred during her bold and very creative escape from Gaskell in Miami.

I don't remember the day she came home. Due to my research, I now know it was just before my 4th birthday. Vague fragments of situations I recall must have happened during that time.

For instance, the Watts family would come up from Terre Haute, Indiana, for summer visits to their Gramma. The elder matriarch lived in a red brick apartment building just south of our house at 5414 S. Ridgewood Court. I was taking a shower in the white rusty metal shower stall in our basement when Tom Watts, my age and the oldest of three sons, came by to play. Ma was doing laundry with the noisy white wringer washer. He came downstairs while I was getting dressed. We went to Tom's Gramma's apartment and visited with his two brothers, Ronnie and Gary. Gramma Watts made this great smelling popcorn that tasted very different from what we usually had. We came back to our house and sat on the front porch swing to devour the treat. It was obviously a great day for me to become such a vivid memory. Well, it must have been the popcorn. They stayed in Chicago for a couple weeks and went back home. I cannot remember how many summer visits they made after that or if they ever found out about Ma's troubles.

My Aunt Stella would come over often and talk to Ma. We would go visit Gramma Wills, who shared an apartment with Stella two blocks away. Aunt Stella had white rabbits and grew tomatoes in the backyard. I could never understand a word Gramma Wills said due to her very thick Polish accent. "Leddy" was Larry and "milluk" was milk, et cetera. Flo, Helen and Stella did not learn Polish during their stay at the boarding school. They communicated with their mom using some version of the English language interspersed with Polish phrases they had assimilated over the years like *"Nie mowic po polsku"* (roughly translated "I do not speak Polish").

Everyone was surprised when Ma showed up. She may have made a phone call home to announce her imminent return but none of us remembers that. I'm sure the watermelons were joyfully received by all except for Mr. Baran who could not have been very excited to see his wildly wayward wife. Ma surely had some " 'splainin' " to do in order to convince Dad to let her stay. Well, correction: Ma probably made it clear what her intentions were.

Ma's getaway car looked very much like this ad from 1951.
Courtesy Don Boyd

Their "conversations" were generally at speeding subway-train decibel levels. Ma had the upper hand in the loudness department. She could shriek with the force of a thousand banshees rising up from the bowels of hell. Well, maybe just a dozen or so banshees. But, I guarantee you, it was loud! Walter could belt-it-out too but not with the mega wattage Flo was able to generate. Nicola Tesla would have been impressed. I can recall us younger ones in the house upstairs behind closed doors hiding under blankets trying to shut out the aural assaults or escaping the cacophony of marital discord to the freedom of the front yard, the safety of the playground across the street or to the sanctuary of Jackson Park and its tranquil lagoon.

Eventually, an uneasy peace settled in. My mother had just broken off a 7-month absence and, what, dad should just welcome her back? Hmmm. Probably not, ya think? Whatever the mood, she *was* back. I wonder how he responded when (if) he found out ma had actually married Gaskell in Las Vegas. I doubt Flo breathed one syllable on that point. Just leave the past behind and hope there is nothing here to fear in the rear-view mirror. Unfortunately for my mother, something *was* definitely in the rear-view mirror for her to fear.

The Sarasota Florida newspaper headline read on June 12 1954;

"Local Robbery Suspect Held"

and June 17, 1954;

"Alleged Robber Of Café Is Held"

and on June 17, 1954;

"Holdup Suspect Is Returned From Miami"

and, on June 23, 1954;

"Theater Gunman Nabbed In Miami For Ritz Holdup"

Courtesy of the Sarasota Herald-Tribune and Sarasota Journal Copyright 1954

Of course, mama never saw any of the newspaper articles about her *Flo*-rida handiwork. She was safely back in the white picket fenced yard calmly petting her collie. Let's give credit where credit is due. Citizen Florence had done her part to restore Law-and-Order in the Deep South. Excellente trabajo Senora! Bravo Mrs. Baran! Way-to-go, Flo!

Bill was in custody. A woman had turned him in. It was reported that she "*spilled the beans*" on him for reasons not made clear. Flo blew his cover by informing the Dade County Sheriff that Abbott was really Gaskell. He faced parole violations in Alabama. There was a fugitive warrant for his arrest because he, as Abbott, ignored the December, 1953, appointment with his Chicago parole officer. Of course, he was also suspected of multiple robberies in Miami, Miami Beach, Panama City, Sarasota and Tallahassee.

Florida States Attorney, W. Mack Smiley, was going to have first crack at Bill. Smiley contacted the Alabama Department of Corrections to inform them of his prize catch. Correspondence from Alabama DOC included the revealing line "*...our William Abbott, your William Gaskell...*" Alabama agreed to let Florida take care of prosecuting Gaskell. They asked that Smiley keep them informed of the on-going events.

Sarasota Herald-Tribune

SARASOTA HERALD-TRIBUNE JUNE 12, 1954

Local Robbery Suspect Held

Lt. Walter Whitted of the city police reported yesterday that a man wanted in connection with the armed robbery of $832 from Morrison's cafeteria here about 8:30 p.m. March 28 was being held by West Miami police.

West Miami police apprehended the man after they received information he was in that town, Lt. Whitted said. He was identified as William Gaskell, about 33-34-years-of-age. He is also wanted in Alabama as a parole violator from the state prison there where he served seven and a half years of a 20 year sentence for armed robbery. St. Petersburg police also have a warrant for his arrest for armed robbery and want him for questioning in connection with another crime, Lt. Whitted said.

Gaskell is also a suspect, police said, for the robbery of the Plaza Restaurant here about 9 p.m. Feb. 7, in which $631 was taken.

Newspaper clipping from 1954.
It was front-page news in Sarasota and St Petersburg.
Courtesy of the Sarasota Herald-Tribune Copyright 1954

94

As a wise guy once said; *a jailbird in the hand is worth two on the loose* (or did I just make that up?). Sorry Bill, game over! The jail at the courthouse on Sarasota's Main Street had a new and exciting guest. Wild Bill Gaskell was now in the custody of the newly elected and highly respected, of whom much was expected Sarasota County Sheriff, Ross Boyer. Boyer had won a close election and was into his second year at the helm of County law enforcement. This was the beginning of what was to become a legendary twenty-year career as the top cop in Sarasota County. But for now, it was the start of a character builder for all involved. Boyer was in for a whole buncha trouble right from the git-go. Nobody said it was going to be easy.

Our anti-hero, number 2, was picked out of this line up of Sarasota County courthouse employees. Notice he is the only one not looking at the camera. Number 7 is G. Dewey Long, a courthouse maintenance man. Soon, Dewey would be mixed up in the middle of this story with the local authorities leveling criminal charges against him.
I'm not sure but did somebody get nervous and wet his pants?
Author's Collection

Sarasota County Sheriff Ross Boyer.
*"So, Mr. Gaskell, could you please identify that
nice-looking dark haired woman driving the get-away car?"*
Photograph courtesy of Sarasota County Historical Resources,
Bill Blackstone Photography Collection

"The first stop was the Cook County Jail....."

July 26th, 1954 was a warm sunny day in Chicago. You can surf the internet weather archives and see for yourself. The beautiful picture that sunny afternoon was about to be shattered for one family on the block.

Bill had just been given up by his pretty pugilistic paramour. He was arrested, delivered to Sarasota County and then thoroughly grilled by US Marshals, the Florida States Attorney and the local Sheriff. Bill returned the favor. After hours of heated questioning, he finally gave up the matron of mayhem. Sarasota's Sheriff Boyer was successful in getting Bill Gaskell to ID the dark-haired gal behind the wheel of the getaway car. Old friends usually know everything about each other: address, phone number, height, weight, kids names, husband's name, where the husband worked ......hmm ...where the husband worked!?!

A Chicago police gathering. The preparations to nab
Florence Baran must have looked like this picture from 1954
Courtesy Special Collections Research Center, University of Chicago Library

There were about 15 Chicago Police, US Marshals and FBI meeting to plan the arrest of an alleged accomplice in multiple armed robberies. I'm wondering how the authorities could have been tipped off as to the schedule and whereabouts of this mother of six? Bill Gaskell was 1200 miles away in the Sarasota County Jail. Would he have known what Flo was up to on a daily basis? It is unlikely that Bill could have or even would have orchestrated this coordinated effort between the Feds and Chicago's finest from a cell in Sarasota.

The authorities had a complication. Bill had warned the Sheriff that he was after a bad-ass and there could be trouble. She could put on a tough-as-nails act and probably would not go quietly. Worst of all, Flo was in the possession of her own .25 caliber Colt pistol purchased on Sarasota's Main Street. Things could get tricky.

Flo had done a poor job of hiding her weapon from the family. My sister Nancy told sister Loretta about a gun she saw. It was stowed away in a second floor heating register. Nancy asked Ma about it. Ma realized she better get that thing out of the house. She did the smart thing but we'll get to that later.

In order to avert a potentially disastrous shoot-out, the lawmen needed some local Chicago reconnaissance to pull off a safe arrest at the home of six children. Why not enlist the husband of the woman in question?

The FBI must have contacted husband Wally at his workplace, Health Food Jobbers in downtown Chicago. There, they explained the facts of the situation. Chicago police and US Marshals must all converge at 5400 South Ridgewood Court at the same time to seize a suspect who might be armed. I wish I could have seen the look on my dad's face when he was told of his wife's nefarious activities. It was bad enough that she ran off with this guy. Now Wally discovers that she is party to a series of coast-to-coast armed robberies. The authorities tell a shocked and dismayed Walter that his wife of sixteen years drove a getaway car in felonious incidents from Illinois to California and back across country ending up in Florida. To top it off, she might have a loaded weapon in the house.

They explained that Florence had a gun with her when she spilled the beans on Gaskell in Miami. She returned home probably still packing heat. They could not predict how Flo would react when confronted by police. The last thing anyone needed was a shootout with a bunch of kids around in a crowded neighborhood across the street from a playground. Not good public relations, that's for sure. It was imperative that they plan carefully and proceed with caution.

Once he found out the details of his spouse's extramarital extracurricular excommunicate-able activities, Walter was happy to help.

This scenario is total conjecture on my part but, after studying the facts and timeline, nothing else makes sense. She left Wally for Wild Bill, the young stud and ne'er-do-well. Now, it's time for penance. This was going to be sweet revenge. Say your prayers, Flo - game over. Wally could have easily disabled the wringer washing machine in the basement. Flo would then have to take the laundry out of the house. A phone call home to Flo from Wally confirms that she is taking a trip to the local laundromat. A phone call to the FBI from Wally at work is the signal to stand by. A well-planned ambush would greet Ma as she casually loaded bags of laundry into her car.

The radios were all on the same frequency. a dozen cars poised at the ready, engines idling, waiting for the command to pounce. There she was, walking towards her car, not suspecting a thing. It would have been better if she didn't have her young boy with her but she had to be taken now. The urgent command blared from the speakers. They moved quickly. Tires squealed and car doors slammed. They got their woman.

After her brawl with five lawmen, my mother was introduced to the concept of incarceration. The first stop was the Cook County Jail at 26th street and California Avenue on Chicago's south side. After the paperwork was done, she was locked in a holding cell where she was exceptionally noisy and uncooperative. Of course she was angrily insisting innocence on her part. The FBI contacted Sheriff Boyer back in Sarasota informing him that the accomplice was in custody, wrestled off the mean streets of Chicago in a violent encounter.

Three days later, Sheriff Boyer and Deputy John Townsend boarded a flight from Tampa to Chicago's Midway airport. Sheriff's wife, Catherine, accompanied them. Mrs. Boyer was acting as matron, a requirement when dealing with a female prisoner. FBI agents briefed the visiting dignitaries. The next step was to get ma onto a flight to face the proverbial music. She was still raging in her cell when the visitors arrived from Florida.

Wally now had to tell his siblings and his mother about the big mess that had just been dumped in his lap. Let's review.

1. She has an affair.
2. She leaves him and the kids for seven months.
3. She suddenly reappears and Wally takes her back.
4. The FBI pays Wally a visit to let him know that his wife is wanted as accomplice in multiple armed robberies.
5. Law enforcement arrests Flo who fights like a snared tigress.
6. The wayward wife is now in jail spitting razor blades at the cops.

What kind of tornado did he marry, anyway? There were incredible conversations and much gnashing of teeth when Walter had to explain the messy details to his brothers, sisters and mother. My father must have done a great acting job in front of us kids in order to look surprised when telling us of ma's predicament. He had to leave out the part where he helped plan the arrest. Our neighbors who witnessed the commotion that day had plenty of fuel for the local gossip machine. There was this girl on our block, about 12 years old with the last name of McCarthy. A few weeks later, I talked to her mentioning ma's vacation. She taunted me saying that *"your mother is in jail"*. I was sure she was not in jail. Why would my mother be in jail? I was told ma was on vacation. I believed what my sisters told me. Jail did not compute.

I cannot recall anything else of that day. The vivid scene of police dragging my mother away was probably enough recollection. Maybe I should try hypnosis to help dig out details submerged in my memory. Loretta watched the commotion outside through the front room window. She froze with a combination of shock and awe and did not understand what she was witnessing. She saw her little brother Freddie run out with his baseball bat to rescue his squirming mother in the clutches of strangers. My sister Jeanne was upstairs in her bedroom reading a book when all this went down. She had no idea that anything happened until Loretta ran upstairs to tell her. By then a police tow truck was hooking up the '51 Chevy, impounding it as evidence. We have no idea exactly where or when Ma got that car. It may have been stolen or legally purchased with the illegal cash. I guess that means it was a stolen car.

Sometime over the next few weeks, I overheard a conversation between Wally and my sisters. My father said the name "Florence Gaskell". I was puzzled by that, not really knowing what they were talking about. Did he know she actually married Bill or did Wally think Gaskell was just an alias? We'll never know the answer to that one.

What about Flo's gun? The police did not find it. I am sure of that. How can I be sure? Fifty-two years later, I found it. We'll save that discussion for later.

Sheriff Boyer's briefcase. His paperwork was well protected when
he made the round-trip flight between Tampa and Chicago.
Author's Collection

      As luck would have it, a few years ago, I received an email from
Robert Snell, a retired Sarasota Sheriff's Deputy. I had purchased a copy
of his book *The History of the Sarasota County Sheriff's Department*.
The book contains a short version of my mother's story as well as a
picture of her being photographed for her mug shot. Deputy Snell
informed me that a woman had the original line-up pic with Bill Gaskell
for sale on EBAY. I contacted her, told her who I was and obtained the
picture which is now in this book. She also had Sheriff Boyer's briefcase
obtained from a garage sale probably conducted by a Boyer family
member. I wasted no time negotiating a price for such a priceless artifact
which also contained some paperwork. I was ecstatic when that package
arrived from Florida. What a find!

TRIAL AND CONVICTION IN SARASOTA

"……..it could not have been plainer that he did not belong there."

The Sarasota Herald Tribune and other local newspapers had a spike in readership in 1954 and 1955 thanks to the exciting adventures of Flo and Bill. This was front-page news back then for the little gulf shore town. The papers carefully recorded the daily events starting in June and leading up to their trial on November 8, 1954, and its aftermath.

Sarasota Herald-Tribune print shop 1955
*Photograph courtesy of Sarasota County Historical Resources,
Bill Blackstone Photography Collection*

In August 1954, Tampa area newspapers began reporting that a woman from Chicago had been arrested and was being accused of acting as a lookout in several daring holdups. She was the accomplice of a man who had been held in Sarasota since June.

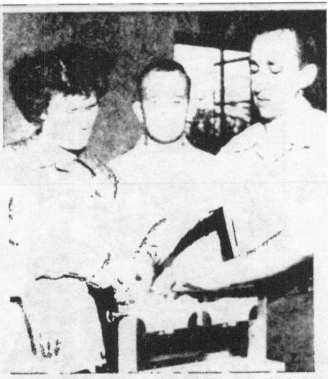

Sarasota Herald-Tribune

SARASOTA, FLORIDA, TUESDAY MORNING, AUGUST 3, 1954

SUSPECT FINGERPRINTED — Deputy Sheriffs George Spanos (left) and Norman Landers fingerprint Florence Gaskell, 35-year-old Chicago woman implicated in two Sarasota holdups last spring. The woman, arrested in Chicago on warrant made by city police, is charged with aiding and abetting an armed robbery. Authorities allege she acted as "lookout" for William Howard Gaskell, also in jail, while he held up a local restaurant and cafeteria for about $1,400.

Courtesy Sarasota Herald Tribune Copyright 1954

It's a hot and steamy August in 1954. Flo and Bill are guests of the Sarasota County Sheriff and the taxpayers of the fine state of Florida. Bill has been lodging there since his June arrest courtesy of Flo's timely tips to the Miami lawmen when *"she spilled the beans for reasons not made clear"*. Now, thanks to *his* timely tips to the Sarasota lawmen, Bill is joined by his "wife" of five months in the Jail at 2000 Main Street.

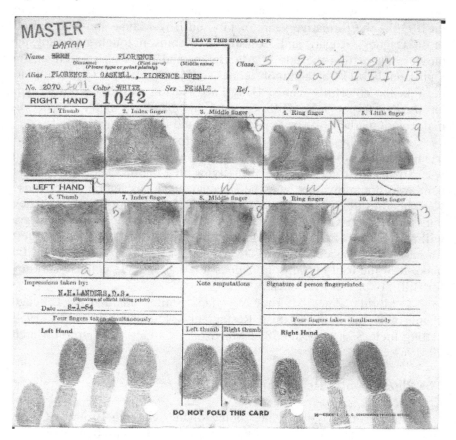

Florence Baran's original fingerprint card from August 1, 1954.
Author's Collection

His current situation paralleled the good old days back on Government Street in Mobile, Alabama, nine years ago. Now he's back in court just like in Mobile, Alabama, nine, years ago. Now he is being charged with multiple counts of armed robbery just like in Mobile, Alabama, nine years ago. You think he'd find some other line of work. Apparently, some habits are hard to break. Maybe he'll beat the rap this time. Maybe Ma-Flo-of-six-kids will beat the rap. Maybe the Chicago Cubs will win the World Series. Holeee Cow! They did!

105

AUTHOR'S TIME OUT! *"Come on, ma, what were you thinking when you ran off with this guy? Bigamy! Larceny! Robbery! Adultery! Abandonment! No matter how you try to sugar coat it, this is bad stuff. Ma had a wild streak in her, ya think?"* Rant over. Thank you for your patience.

There were plenty of negative role models to go around during the 1930's, the formative years of Flo and Bill. Maybe she watched all those Cagney, Bogart and Edward G. Robinson tough-guy gangster movies. There was the tale of Ma Barker and her sons as well as the highly publicized Chicago mobsters as well as Bonnie and Clyde. Add to the mix the colorfully named Baby-Face Nelson and Pretty-boy Floyd; let us not forget John Dillinger and his band of merry murdering malevolent marksmen – or - maybe we should fuggedabowd-em!

According to the FBI, two men from Miami visited Chicago trying to raise Bill's bail money. One man, identified as Oscar McCurdy, was a parolee from Alabama then living in Miami. The other man's name was not known but he owned or managed a gas station there. These were buddies of Bill that he met during his Alabama prison days. They must have been very good friends - birds of a feather - if they were willing to travel to Chicago to gather funds for Bill's defense. The quest for cash was unsuccessful. Bill never made bail although his mother did make it to the trial in Sarasota. Agnes hired a Sarasota defense attorney for Bill.

Florida States Attorney W. Mack Smiley charged the Chicago couple with the Plaza Spanish Restaurant holdup on February 7, 1954 netting them $531 and the $832 Morrison's Cafeteria holdup on March 20, 1954.

The Plaza Spanish Restaurant Holdup

Sarasota was the winter home of the Ringling Brothers Circus and the spring training home of the Boston Red Sox baseball team. The renowned Ringling Art Museum was a magnet for the rich, the famous, and fat cats of all persuasions. With all this wealth in the neighborhood, Bill was looking forward to raking in some easy money. By this time, he's an ice cold pro at his chosen profession, all grown up since the Alabama days. No longer an immature 18 year-old stick-up artist, now he was an immature 27 year-old stick-up artist, settled in his ways for better or for worse, still doin' the crime and still doin' the time.

The Plaza Spanish Restaurant was an upscale venue. It was about 9 PM and the restaurant was host to about 40 diners. Bill made his appearance there on the evening of February 7, 1954. Manager Randy Hagerman thought he looked out of place. *"Even if he had a sign on his back, it could not have been plainer that he did not belong there.....He was rough looking.*" His clothes were several steps down the social ladder from the finery that cloaked the regular Plaza clientele.

The aroma of Carne Asada on the grill filled the air as Bill approached the cashier, Mrs. Pauline Williams. Knowing that the sound of tinkling wine glasses and the din of dinner conversation would provide cover for his intent, he flashed his best Bill smile and calmly requested change for a dollar. When she opened the cash register, this time Bill flashed his gun and calmly demanded, *"Give it to me"*. He grabbed the cash and made his dash out the front door. Witnesses reported that he jumped into a running car with a dark-haired woman at the wheel. The police arrived within minutes but the perilous pair was long gone. The cashier went into hysterics after Bill ran out. Mrs. Williams was so distraught that she had to be taken home. The authorities could not question her until she calmed down.

The County Sheriff, Venice police and the Florida Highway Patrol all joined in the search to no avail. Nearby Highway US 41, also known as the Tamiami Trail, was their probable escape route. It connects Sarasota with Miami. Many know it by its other name; "Alligator Alley" where it travels east/west through the Everglades swamp.

They got away with this stick up and continued their pirate party throughout Florida. However, when it came time to ID a suspect in the Plaza robbery, no one could positively identify Bill. Much to the disappointment of States Attorney Smiley, he had no choice but to dismiss the charges.

November 3, 1954 Sarasota Journal article starts with:

CIRCUIT COURT SET TO OPEN HERE NEXT MONDAY

"*........ Other cases set for next week: Monday, William H. Gaskell and Florence Gaskell, charged with robbery........*"

The Morrison's Cafeteria Holdup

The trial started on Monday, November 8th, 1954. Many witnesses came forth for the Morrison's job to help describe the scene of the crime for the half-dozen jurors.

It's dinner time at Morrison's. The place was packed, which, in armed robbery terms, is synonymous with mucho cash available for the taking. Miss Violet Piggens was the cashier when Bill strolled in. He entered like any other customer and had a nice meal. Wild Bill sat down, enjoyed his southern fried chicken (my guess) while looking around and casing the joint. The scene met with his approval. It was gonna be the proverbial piece of cake. Right after he finished eating his piece of cake, he got in line with other patrons to pay for the meal. *This* dinner was going to be on-the-house. When Bill's turn came, Miss Piggens claimed that he pulled out the gun and turned his body at an angle to hide the weapon from other patrons in line behind him. Violet gave Bill a stack of paper money. It wasn't enough. With a menacing stare, he quietly ordered her to *"Give me all of it!"*

Morrison's Cafeteria eventually closed and the building became the Golden Apple Dinner Theatre. On March 20, 1954, Bill Gaskell sprinted through that alley to a waiting car on the next block.
Author's Collection

She complied and emptied the cash register. Bill calmly walked out of the restaurant, looked around, then sprinted thru the alley adjacent to the building. Morrison's janitor, Horace King, was reporting for work at that moment. He testified that he saw Bill running in the alley towards the next block. As usual, Flo was there waiting with the engine running. Bill hopped in and off they went. The total take for Flo and Bill was $832. Adjusted for inflation, that is about $9,000 today. Time to buy some beer!

Mrs. Jules Lancer was proprietor of the little Sarasota pawn shop at 1545 Main Street. Jules Surplus Store was also known as Jules Pawn and Music Center. As of this writing, it is now the Stakenborg Art Gallery.

Mrs. Lancer testified that Florence bought a .25 caliber Colt pistol at the store on March 17, 1954. This was three days before the Morrison's job. Bill was caught with same type of gun but the serial number did not match the weapon sold to Flo. Where was Flo's gun? It was hiding out with her sister Stella back in Chicago.

November 9, 1954, Sarasota Journal article starts with:

Bandit, Girlfriend Guilty Of Robbery

November 9, 1954, Sarasota Herald-Tribune article starts with:

Man, Woman Convicted On Robbery Count

The six-person jury found Bill guilty of first-degree armed robbery. Flo was found guilty of second-degree armed robbery, also known as aiding and abetting or accessory to armed robbery. Incredibly, Flo always claimed that she had no knowledge of what Bill was up to when she was waiting in the car for him. She was just patiently sitting in the car, humming her favorite tune, minding her own business, lah-tee-dah. Nice try ma. Once again, what were you thinking?

November 25, 1954, Sarasota Herald-Tribune article starts with:

Morrison's Cafeteria Bandit Gets 15 Year Sentence

It's Thursday, November 25, 1954; Happy Thanksgiving everybody and especially those six kids back in Chicago. The Sarasota newspaper reports that, on Wednesday, Judge W. T. Harrison sentenced Bill to 15 years hard time at Raiford State Prison. Bill heard the bad news after he made a long statement in his own defense. *"My mother paid $250 for the lawyer and he only came to see me twice,"* Bill claimed. *"If I could have had more time I could have produced witnesses to prove I was in Tampa at the time of the stickup."* I don't know Bill. You were there since June. Not enough time for your attorney to take care of business?

Gaskell then berated a newspaper reporter for "inferring" that Flo was a "loose woman". He went on to explain that they were going together after his parole from the Alabama prison where he had served seven years for armed robbery. *"....and the only reason I didn't marry her (earlier) was because I was on parole and her husband was trying to have us arrested."*

109

Gaskell made a point of the fact that he had *"...spent $12.50 to get married in Las Vegas."* He continued, *"Well, of course, we committed bigamy but I did marry her. That ought to show I thought a lot of her."*

Florence then appeared before the judge. She took the opportunity to make a statement. Her speech was described as *"... long, halted and at times incoherent."* She denied admitting any crimes to Sheriff Boyer and his wife when they returned her from Chicago.

Colt .25 caliber semiautomatic pistol,
the intimidator of choice for Flo and Bill
Author's Collection

She then states that her husband approved of her leaving Chicago with Bill for the cross country amorous get-away. *"Well he didn't exactly give me permission. He gave me an excuse. He was going to have us arrested."* Wally eventually had her charged with desertion.

Judge Harrison then made the point that he would not sentence Florence at this time pending charges elsewhere. It could take a while because of the many warrants for the pair on file from California to Florida.

Florida States Attorney W. Mack Smiley
His portrait hangs in the Sarasota States Attorney office.
Author's Collection

Before he began serving his 15-year sentence, Bill got a police escort to Tallahassee to stand trial for two theater heists, one in Panama City and the other in Tallahassee. In the meantime, Flo remained under the watchful eye of Sheriff Boyer at the County Jail, often called the "Boyer Bastille" by the locals.

Judge W.T. Harrison. His portrait hangs in the new
Sarasota County Courthouse.
Author's Collection

Ma could not have been too happy about the way this whole thing turned out. Gone were the days of swinging on the front porch with big band music wailing from the old Zenith radio. Gone were the placid moments admiring the collie dog lounging in the shade of the triple-trunk Sumac tree in the yard surrounded by the white picket fence with her three-year-old boy lying on the cool lawn, petting Lassie's tan head. Gone were the days of family outings at the Indiana Dunes with her sister Stella. Gone were the days of hubby Wally winning foot races up the steep sand dunes against Stella's boyfriend, George Livermore. Gone were the days of the softly glowing Christmas tree that adorned the Ridgewood Court front room, with flashes and sparkles from tinsel, ornaments and lights, illuminating the Nativity scene below. Gone were the days of 120 decibel screaming matches with Wally for little things like leaving the plastic wrap on the Thanksgiving Day turkey when the dumb cluck (her words) put it in the oven to roast at 400 degrees. Ah, yes, sweet memories all.

"All rise. The honorable Judge W.T. Harrison presiding".
The refurbished Courtroom on the main floor of the County Courthouse.
Author's Collection

Mrs. Florence. Baran covers her face as she leaves the Circuit Court room yesterday, with Deputy Sheriff Lonnie Selph, after her conviction for complicity in the holdup of Morrison's Cafeteria here last August. She and her boy friend, William Gaskell, were convicted by a jury and now await sentencing by Judge W. T. Harrison.

"Mrs. Florence Baran covers her face as she leaves the Circuit Court room yesterday, with Deputy Sheriff Lonnie Selph, after her conviction for complicity in the holdup of Morrison's Cafeteria here last (March) *August. She and her boyfriend, William Gaskell, were convicted by a jury and now await sentencing by Judge W.T. Harrison.*

114

"TRAILS END - *William H. Gaskell, 27, parole convict, is led from circuit court yesterday after being found guilty of the holdup robbery of Morrison's Cafeteria last March 28. Leading him from the courtroom are Deputies Dick Curry, center, and John Townsend. Also found guilty to a charge of being an accomplice to the crime was Gaskell's girlfriend, Mrs. Florence Baran, right, who deserted her husband and six children in Chicago to accompany the gunman on a cross-country crime spree that extended from California to Florida.*"

Courtesy Sarasota Herald-Tribune Copyright 1954

115

Bandit Convicted

William H. Gaskell, 27, (center) is shown with his mother and Deputy Sheriff John Townsend as he leaves the circuit court room yesterday following his conviction on charges of holding up Morrison's Cafeteria here last March. The Gaskells are from Chicago. Judge W. T. Harrison will pronounce sentence later.

"William H. Gaskell, 27, (center) is shown with his mother and Deputy Sheriff John Townsend as he leaves the courtroom yesterday following his conviction on charges of holding up Morrison's Cafeteria here last March. The Gaskells are from Chicago. Judge W. T. Harrison will pronounce sentence later. "

Now we have steel bars caging in this wild "womanimal". She punctuated her stay at the jail with fits of anger directed at the deputies and the legal system that slammed the door on her freedom. Sometimes she would complain loudly and keep other inmates up at night with singing and harmonica playing. *They let her have her harmonica in the county jail?* That was nice of them. There were reports of dear Flo damaging plumbing and ripping off her clothes during fits of rage. Did *that* convince anyone of her innocence? Every prisoner *is* innocent, right? Just ask them.

116

A restored section of the Sarasota County Courtroom.
The well-traveled posteriors of Flo and Bill graced
fine padded chairs like these on November 8, 1954.

Author's Collection

Main street in Sarasota in the 1950's. This is the scene
enjoyed by Flo and Bill during their vacation together.

Photograph courtesy of Sarasota County Historical Resources,
Bill Blackstone Photography Collection

THE GREAT ESCAPE

"She's cunning, she's smart and she's mean. She'll lick any ordinary man."

I'm guessing that relatively few mothers have ever been convicted of second-degree armed robbery. Accessory to armed robbery is not the worst thing a mama could be but that reputation, along with that adultery thing, would certainly minimize her chances of being named Mother-Of-The-Year. Granted, Florence was not a serial killer, axe murderess, child molester or celebrity chef; dangerous characters all! She just drove a getaway car while belligerent Bill provided the muscle for their day-to-day spending money. He was acting as front man of a latter-day PG version of Bonnie and Clyde.

Let's not get all carried away with the obvious comparison to B & C. To their "credit", F & B never pulled the trigger and nobody was ever hurt. Plenty of hurt feelings? Of course. Many frightened cashiers and terrorized employees were first-person witnesses to their handiwork. Most victims had never witnessed the business end of a gun before. Then there were the legions of frustrated law enforcement officials from sea to shining sea trying to put an end to a well-documented cross-country robbery tour.

Ma assisted authorities by attempting to write her own end to the story when she split from Bill at that Miami motel. She turns in a public nuisance and returns to Chicago to make amends with the family. The Housewife was sure she was home free. She could not have envisioned how the tale of Flo and Bill would develop from there.

On January 19th of 1955, Florence was impatiently awaiting sentencing at the Sarasota County jail. Judge W.T. Harrison received word that my mother would not stand trial for the two theater robberies in Leon County. He was satisfied that she was off the streets and would soon be on her way to the state prison.

In Sarasota, Bill received a sentence of 15-years confinement at the Raiford State Prison. Now he was being prosecuted for a theater hold up in Panama City, which occurred on April 4th, 1954. There, the newly wedded pair netted $460 in cash.

If Flo and Bill still wanted to make a splash in the movies, this was as close as they were gonna get - theater lobby cash registers. You gotta start somewhere, I suppose.

Next, Flo learns her fate.

Wednesday, January 19, 1955, the Sarasota Herald Tribune headline read:

Woman Gets 10 Years For Part In Robbery

"Mrs. Florence Baran, who was convicted last Nov. 8 of aiding and abetting in the robbery of Morrison's Cafeteria here, was sentenced to 10 years in the state women's penitentiary when she appeared before Judge W. T. Harrison yesterday. The judge had withheld sentencing while waiting to determine what action would be taken by other states and counties where she is wanted for similar crimes."

Courtesy Sarasota Herald-Tribune Copyright 1955

Hmmm, ten years confinement in the woman's section of Raiford State Prison - taxpayer subsidized room and board. Given that she had always denied any knowledge of Bill's crimes and insisted on her innocence, she was particularly outraged at the sentence. She fully expected to get a few years of court supervision or probation. Indignation ruled her thoughts. *"How dare they arrest and imprison a married mother of six children".*

Sheriff Boyer knew she was a handful *before* sentencing. Things deteriorated in a hurry. Ma's county jail cell evolved into an angry hornet's nest. She resurrected her noisy wench act by banging on the walls and throwing pillows and other sundry items at the bars of her cell while cursing out deputies and courthouse staff whenever they passed by.

3AM, Sunday morning, January 23, 1955; Flo had an easy time of it. She cut a hole in the ceiling, climbed up with her packed suitcase, made her way though the darkened attic, found the access hatch, descended the ladder into a closet inside the grand jury room, opened a door leading to the 2nd floor hallway, tiptoed down the stairs and opened freedom's door to Main Street. After a cautious glance and a deep breath, she calmly strolled into the cool humid Florida night.

7AM, Sunday morning, January 23, 1955; Sheriff Deputies made the usual morning bed checks. Surprise! Surprise! Her cell was empty. A 2-foot diameter hole in the ceiling above Flo's cot attracted the deputy's attention. The hole led to the jailhouse attic, an unlit cavern full of pipes, electrical wiring and bare rafters supporting the heavy clay tile roof of the Sarasota County Courthouse.

While up in the attic, Flo followed the light coming from an access hatch in the grand jury room closet. Someone had left the closet light on. Coincidence? She lifted the hatch and saw the permanently installed steel ladder attached to the wall. Flo climbed down, but left the attic access hatch open and the closet light on. Imagine her excitement as she contemplated the journey back home. Her heart was pounding as she carefully lowered herself down the metal rungs. One slip, sneeze or cough and its back to her cell with an attempted escape charge on her head. Yeah, well, she showed those dummies. *"I'm outa here!"*

Once outside, she stuck out a hitchhikers thumb hoping to catch a ride away from her tormenters at the county jail. She was picked up by some helpful souls who must have heard a convincing story from this lady in distress at 3 o'clock in the morning. Flo had to think fast in order to explain her early morning presence on Main Street. I wonder what she told them.

"My car broke down. Will you help me?"
"My car was stolen. Will you help me?"
"My husband kicked me out of the house. Will you help me?"
"I just broke out of the county jail over there and need a ride to escape to Chicago to rejoin my husband and six kids. Will you help me?"

Her benefactors had been out drinking late Saturday night. When they saw my mother with her outstretched hand, they responded to the milk of human kindness flowing through their veins. Maybe it was just the Budweiser flowing through their veins. Anyway, they took dear old mom to their place in Tampa where she spent the night. Elated by her lucky break, she celebrated her hard-earned freedom with a few beers.

The next day back in Chicago, my aunt Stella gets a long distance phone call. It probably went something like this;

"Hi Stella. I just broke out of jail. Yeah, really, just like in the movies. I'm still in Florida. I'm staying in Tampa. Say, can you wire me $50 for bus fare? I remember robbing...uh, I mean, visiting a Western Union in town so send it there. I probably should not use my name for obvious reasons. Address it to Helen Hawthorne. Our little sister won't mind if I assume her identity just this once. She's an understanding soul and still owes me a favor for all those extra desserts I stole for her back in boarding school. I'm taking the Greyhound bus home. Thanks dear. Love you! See you soon. Bye Bye, Bye".

Great plan! Ma has some cash, a ticket to ride and a newfound wicked sense of humor. While picking up the money at the Western Union, she gets the idea to send a little greeting back to the hard working public servant Sheriff Boyer – a parting shot, if you will.

The telegram read something like:

"Having a great time. Wish you were here!"

She apparently had a flair for comedy when the situation called for it. But ma, should you really be rubbing the Sheriff's nose in it like that? He was just doing his job, clearing the streets of pathological public enemies, sinful scruffy scofflaws and other voracious virulent vermin. If nothing else, Boyer should be glad the jailhouse would finally have some silent nights with Fist Fightin' Flo out of the picture.

Flo quietly tip-toed as she descended this jailhouse stairway
during her escape at 3AM on Sunday, January 23, 1955.

Author's Collection

122

SARASOTA, FLORIDA, MONDAY MORNING, JANUARY 24, 1955

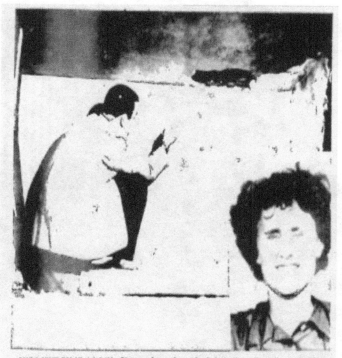

SHE WENT THAT-A-WAY—Picture above shows the hole in the ceiling above the second-floor cell block at the Sarasota county jail through which a woman sentenced to 10 years in prison for her role in an armed robbery made her escape early yesterday morning. Inset at lower right is a picture of the escapee, Mrs. Florence Baran, 36.

Hey Sheriff, look who's smiling now! *"SHE WENT THAT-A-WAY - Picture above shows the hole in the ceiling above the 2nd floor cell block at the Sarasota county jail through which a woman sentenced to 10 years in prison for her role in an armed robbery made her escape early yesterday morning. Inset at lower right is a picture of the escapee, Mrs. Florence Baran, 36.*

Monday Morning, January 24, 1955, the headline read:

Woman Escapes From Local Jail

DEPUTY SHERIFF Lonnie Selph points to the bunk in the county jail which had been occupied by Florence Baran, who escaped yesterday. Arrow in upper left corner shows spot behind the steel caging where the convicted robbery accomplice cut a hole through the ceiling. The door behind Selph had been open.

Photograph courtesy of Sarasota County Historical Resources,
Bill Blackstone Photography Collection

Tuesday Morning, January 25, 1955, the headline read:

Sheriff Seeks Woman Escapee

The steel ladder leading to the attic of the county jail used by
my mom for her daring escape. The ladder was in a hallway
outside the Grand Jury room which gave access
to a stairway to the courthouse corridor.

Photograph courtesy of Sarasota County Historical Resources,
Bill Blackstone Photography Collection

These 1955 Ford station wagons made fine patrol cars
for the Sheriff's department. Flo ducked for cover
whenever she saw these bad boys on the street.

Photograph courtesy of Sarasota County Historical Resources,
Bill Blackstone Photography Collection

By this time, sheriff wanted to turn the "woman escapee" over his knee and administer some corrective action, a therapeutic spanking of Biblical proportions no doubt. Of course, the Sarasota Herald Tribune was getting plenty of fodder for its daily paper, much at the expense of Boyer's reputation. I can imagine the snickering in the pressroom when the next thing popped up.

Wednesday Morning, January 26, 1955, the headline read:

Jailhouse Romance Of Youth, Florence Bared

Noisy wench or Polish bunny? The excitement in Sarasota was really building now. The original article explains it best. I need to transcribe it here for you in its entirety courtesy of the Sarasota Herald-Tribune.

"Clues to the whereabouts of jail breaking Florence Baran, 36, remained discouragingly absent yesterday; however the day did yield definite proof that others outside the realm of law enforcement yearn to lay hands on her. Not that they expect it to entice her to return here, but Sheriff Ross E. Boyer and his deputies would like her to know that an interesting item of mail has arrived.

Contents of her letter indicate she is sought as eagerly for her amorous accomplishments as for her talents in jail breaking. The letter addressed to the Chicago mother of six came from a 15-year-old Ohio boy who occupied a cell adjoining hers for more than two weeks. Welfare authorities finally returned the boy to his home in Ohio but the letter he wrote revealed that he left his heart in Sarasota.

The cells in the women's section of the county jail are adjacent to those occupied by juveniles. When the boy was picked up here as a runaway, he found himself confined to what he considered an exceedingly superior jail.

To the rest of the inmates Mrs. Baran was a "noisy wench" who had been convicted and sentenced to a 10 year prison term for being an accomplice to armed robbery. But to the boy she was his first love.

In his letter he referred to her as "my Polish bunny" and wrote longingly of those glamorous nights in the jailhouse. Amid this atmosphere of hearts and flowers he assured the 175-pound Chicagoan that his love bloomed fully and remained undying.

Coyly he confessed that she had administered his first real kiss and further sultry recollections caused deputies to ponder the possible extent to which jailhouse romancing can go.

The boy's love for Florence was so mighty that it was assumed he could even tolerate her nocturnal harmonica playing – an infestation that caused other prisoners to complain that the local calaboose was losing its reputation for being a reputable resort.

After penning a sonnet wherein the general theme was that he would like to latch on to her and hold her tight, the boy assured Florence that as soon as the school year ends in June he will hasten to Chicago to join her in playing house.

The boy, like Florence, was operating under the highly erroneous assumption that when Judge W. T. Harrison passed sentence on her January 18 he would deal her nothing worse than a slight case of probation. The judge however was dealing from a vastly different deck – this being a turn of events that caused Florence to rise to extreme indignation.

As final proof that his love is great the boy assured Florence that once he joined her in housekeeping he would lend his assistance to any project she cared to launch in extracting her previous light-of-love from the interior of Raiford Penitentiary.

127

This rival in the pursuit of the affections of Florence is William H. Gaskell, 28, who finds himself in the unpleasant position of being hopelessly in debt to the State of Florida.

Gaskell, who went so far as to marry Florence in bigamous manner, drew 15 years for his part in the holdup that brought them both to grief. He has been transferred to Leon County where authorities have every intention of lathering him with another resounding sentence for persuading money from a Tallahassee cashier by tenderly offering to blow her brains out.

"All we need to get Bill out is plenty of money and you know how to get that," the enraptured boy wrote. He added that "it sure will be fun living with you and Bill."

All of which led authorities to comment that the boy certainly doesn't know much about (1) love, (2) Bill, and (3) Florence.

Courtesy Sarasota Herald-Tribune Copyright 1955

A staff writer for the Herald Tribune, Stan Windhorn, interviewed Flo and Bill several times for his "Sarasota Scene" column. The article, published on Wednesday, January 26 1955, entitled

Two Convicts Have Their Own Law.

It was a thorough examination of the freewheeling felons and their relationship to society. It summarized their actions over the past year by referring to Bill's lack of remorse for the crime spree. Gaskell insisted that since his 1945 Alabama conviction and jail time were 'unjust', he was just making up for lost time by getting as much money as fast as possible by any means necessary. To his way of thinking, he was just getting even with a system that deprived him of seven years of his freedom. The deadly Clyde Barrow made a similar claim in an attempt to justify his crime spree with Bonnie Parker. Bill's only remorse was for being caught.

Bill explained away his bigamous relationship with Florence *"with a vigor that indicated a clear conscience."* Did a marriage ceremony make their association proper and dignified? Gaskell played up the fact that he gladly spent money for the marriage license by stating *"That ought to show you that I thought a lot of Florence".*

Flo also had a few sharp words for Mr. Windhorn. One night she called the writer to her county jail cell to *"berate him in her normal and profane manner".* She complained about his making her sound like a *"loose woman".* She tersely reminded him that she returned to her husband and children in June, 1954. This was clear evidence of her nurturing, responsible and motherly nature.

So, just how did my mother really accomplish her daring nocturnal flight from justice?

A court house employee is a trusted member of the community. So when a trusted member of the community aids in a jail break, it comes as a rude surprise.

Thursday, January 27, 1955, The Sarasota Herald-tribune headline read:

Janitor Held For Aiding In Escape

Sheriff Boyer ain't no dummy. He examined the clues all along the escape route. A prisoner had escaped from the same cell a few years before Flo. Someone must have told ma about the patched-up hole in the ceiling, the access hatch, the ladder and how nice and quiet things were at 3 o'clock in the morning. At that hour, no guards other than two night-shift sheriff deputies were in the building. Deserted hallways and unlocked doors would greet her if she was willing to take the chance. Armed with the reconnaissance provided by Mr. G. Dewey Long, Flo figured, *"What do I have to lose now?"* Another adventure awaits.

She took Dewey's advice and hit the road. Some theorized that this was part of a bigger plan to spring Bill from the Leon County Jail. The sheriff there was put on alert that Flo might make an appearance. I don't know about that theory. Why would she want to get back together with Bill? Didn't she just turn him in to the coppers in Miami? Didn't he rat her out too? Maybe Flo would have wanted to punch him in the nose or knock a few of his screws loose by serving up some blunt force trauma with a large heavy object. Probably not. The caged animal just wanted to return to her natural habitat.

Sheriff Ross Boyer at the radio.
"Be on the lookout for the baddest babe you've ever seen.
Approach with extreme caution and be ready for action"

Photograph courtesy of Sarasota County Historical Resources,
Bill Blackstone Photography Collection

In response to questions about the Chicago woman who beat her way out of her county jail cell, Sheriff Boyer said *"She's cunning, she's smart and she's mean. She'll lick any ordinary man."* Law enforcement officials were warned to exercise extreme caution in apprehending this woman. They never did recover her gun bought the year before at the surplus store on Main Street. Will she have that weapon when lawmen finally catch up with her? And will she use it? The cops had to be careful. Ma demonstrated a highly developed sense of self-preservation in past encounters with law enforcement officials.

Meanwhile, the case against Dewey Long was taking shape. He steadfastly refused to admit any part in the escape. He did consent to taking a lie detector test, along with another courthouse janitor, Sam Jordan. The pair was sent off to Miami where the test equipment was located.

Sam passed with flying colors. Dewey, however, suddenly decided to refuse the test after discussing the operation of the machine with its operator. This red flag along with other circumstantial evidence prompted the immediate booking of Dewey Long into the Sarasota County Jail when he returned from Miami. He had spent many hours over the years cleaning and maintaining the cells. Now he got the chance to experience his jail from a completely new perspective.

The Sheriff and States Attorney were convinced Flo had inside help. Suspicion centered on Long when it was reported by other janitors and deputies that Dewey had spent considerable time near the cell talking to Mrs. Baran. Long had keys to all areas of the courthouse and jail, so it was normal to see him anywhere in the facility. However, it was unusual that he would spend so much time in conversation with her or any other inmate.

Friday Morning, January 28, 1955, The headline read:

Courthouse Janitor Is Discharged By Board

There was growing suspicion that some jailhouse hanky panky between the Baran woman and Dewey may have influenced his decision to furnish her with a piece of lumber, a hammer, a screwdriver and the location of a weak spot in the ceiling. Dewey was 53 years old and Flo was 36. He might have taken a liking to the younger gal. Maybe Flo made him a promise that she was not going keep. Dewey was just the chump she needed to help her return to her Chicago roots.

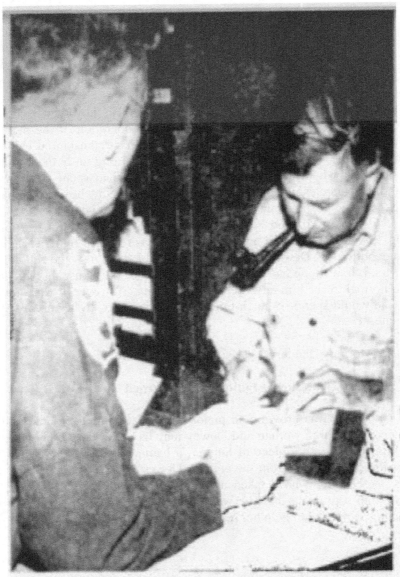

AIDED ESCAPEE?—G. Dewey Long, courthouse janitor, is being booked on charges of aiding Mrs. Florence Baran in making her escape from the local jail. Deputy Sheriff Lonnie Selph is booking Long after an investigation by Sheriff Ross Boyer.

Courtesy Sarasota Herald-Tribune Copyright 1955

Other clues pointed to an accomplice in the escape; a light left on in the attic; the ladder in the grand jury office; the location of the hatch leading to ladder; the weak spot in her cell ceiling where another prisoner made his escape years earlier. How did Flo know about these things? Evidence was piling up for a conviction.

Mr. Long spent less than an hour in jail. A professional bondsman appeared with $2000 and Dewey was on his way home. There he was informed that his name had been removed from the payroll of his beloved Sarasota County. Dewey lost his job over this thing. *"Ya play with far* (sic) *and yer gonna git burned."*

The local media wasted little time in generating copy for the story hungry public. A jail break! Jailhouse romance! Their own little mini-scandal. They had some fun with it.

In a February 6th article, Herald-Tribune writer Paul Einstein reported Sheriff Boyer had just been selected by the local Kiwanis Club as the new song leader at their meetings. Boyer started the next Friday get-together with an attempt to shine the light of humor on the escape, by casually mentioning that he had been requested to sing *The Prisoner Song*. He quipped that this wasn't going to happen and then asked the Kiwanians to sing *I Want a Girl*. The song started but soon spontaneous laughter broke out in the meeting room. Boyer had unknowingly topped his own *Prisoner Song* gag. When the song ended, Boyer commented *"If anyone sees Florence, call me"*.

Meanwhile, Bill's fate is in the hands, hearts and minds of a jury in Tallahassee. The Leon County prosecutor introduced witnesses making this trial the proverbial slam-dunk.

The charges were spelled out in the official court documents;

(In Panama City) *".....did then and there by force, violence or assault, or putting in fear, feloniously rob steal and take from the person or custody of Mrs. N.T. Holland certain property then and there the subject of larceny to wit: four hundred sixty dollars ($460) United States currency......."*

Then there was another theater heist in nearby Tallahassee:

"......on the 29th day of May 1954 with force and arms at and in the county of Leon aforesaid, did then and there by force, violence or assault, or putting in fear, feloniously rob steal and take from the person or custody of T.L. Hyde and B.F. Hyde certain property then and there the subject of larceny to wit: four hundred dollars ($400) United States currency......."

The jury found Bill guilty as charged for two counts of armed robbery. Let's tack on another 20 years of prison time for each count. The tally is now forty more years behind bars for Wild Bill.

Jury note from the Leon County trial, February 1, 1955
"We the jury find the defendant guilty as charged so say we all"
Author's Collection

Sheriff Boyer inspects one of the county jail cells
on the 2nd floor of the courthouse building.

Photograph courtesy of Sarasota County Historical Resources,
Bill Blackstone Photography Collection

Two of the harmonicas belonging to Flo the Fleeing Fugitive.
She preferred the Hohner 64 Chromonica, a top quality 4 octave
chromatic unit, the choice for professionals, semi professionals
and those convicted of accessory to armed robbery. She always
kept two around in case one broke or got lost during a
high speed car chase or while fleeing on foot.
Author's Collection

RETURN TO SARASOTA

"Those Chicago officers were sure glad to get rid of her".

Apparently, my mommy was living under the delusion that she would never be caught again. She must have imagined something like;

"Why would the authorities waste their time with me? They have their man. Bill is the real criminal here. He's going to be locked up for a long time. OK. So I rubbed Sheriff Boyer's face in it with that Tampa-teaser-by-telegram. Sorry about that but I'm sure sheriff and the boys got a big laugh about that. It was just some good-natured ribbing. I'll just lay low here at home for a while until the dust settles. They'll soon forget all about me."

The headline in the Sarasota Journal, April 27, 1955:

Florence Baran Seized By FBI

"Florence Baran, described by Chicago authorities as 'a fighter with a taste for raw garlic' was seized by FBI agents in the windy city yesterday, and Sheriff Ross Boyer, who has taken considerable 'kidding' about her escape several months ago, was one of the first to receive the news...The sheriff had no trouble at all recalling the days when Florence was methodically ripping up cell after cell at the courthouse jail. They (the FBI) said she was 'extremely strong and liked to fight' "

They were in no hurry to apprehend her. It wasn't until three months after the escape that US Marshals finally nabbed her at the Hyde Park Chicago restaurant where she worked as a waitress. Sheriff Boyer was in the Sarasota Herald-Tribune wire room when the word of Florence's arrest came over the Associated Press teletype. Big news for Boyer.

"It was a violent encounter," admitted the FBI describing the events of April 26th, 1955. Three men wrestled the five-foot-eight inch tall 160-pound woman into submission and slapped the cuffs on her. The customers at the eatery must have had a lot to talk about that day! *"I'll have the tuna salad, a bagel and one escaped felon under arrest by US Marshals please."* A tasty meal and an impromptu floor show; way-to-go, Flo!

St. Petersburg Times headline of Thursday, April 28th, 1955 read:

Sheriff Plans To Bring Back Baran Woman

Sheriff Boyer was relieved to hear that Florence was finally under wraps in Chicago. Now he just had to schedule a second trip to return the enigmatic and elusive Mrs. Jail Breaker back to Sarasota.

In the interim, Herald-Tribune columnist Paul Einstein couldn't resist taking one more good-spirited jab at Boyer. In his *Inside Sarasota* column, Einstein described how Florence escaped from the "Boyer Bastille" but was now in the custody of the FBI.

Once again, the sheriff was leading the singing at the Friday night Kiwanis club meeting. Local banker Roger Adams requested that they sing *"Bring Back My Bonnie To Me"*. Before Boyer could react, city Commissioner John Teale took the floor and quipped *"Sing 'Chicago' "*. Boyer gave them all a knowing glance, smiled and sang *"I've Been Working On The Railroad."*

The headline in the Sarasota Journal, April 28th, 1955:

Mrs. Baran Faces Federal Arraignment

The FBI informed Sheriff Boyer that Flo would face arraignment by authorities in Chicago before being released to Sarasota law enforcement. She now had to contest the charge of unlawful flight to avoid confinement. As it turned out, since Florence was already sentenced, the Feds showed some mercy and decided to drop those charges and just let Florida deal with her. She was mired in enough deep doo-doo so there was no need pile it on.

Once again, Ma acquainted herself with the amenities of the Cook County Jail on Chicago's south side. She languished there for a month before Sheriff Boyer, deputy "Big John" Townsend and Mrs. Catherine Boyer made their second trip from Florida to re-embrace her with their long tender arms of the law. Boyer stated with his usual repartee, *"Those Chicago officers sure were glad to get rid of her."*

On May 29, 1955, Ma is welcomed back to the Sarasota County Jail now with heightened security. With the words *"... she's mean, she's tough and she's gonna hurt somebody bad ..."* echoing through the hallways of the county courthouse, they were taking no chances this time. Extreme caution was the order of the day. Sheriff Boyer did not need any more negative press reports or media ribbing, no matter how "good-natured" the negative press or media ribbing appeared to be. This was *serious* business now. The battling babe from Chicago had their attention *big time*.

Sheriff Boyer said he had no trouble with Mrs. Baran on this return trip. *"She was in no mood to talk and I did not encourage her."* He reported there were no *"anxious moments"* before or during the flight but, as expected, she was her usual *"uncooperative"* self. Florence tried to stall around at the airport, attempting to force them to miss the plane to Tampa but they made it on time. Her usually reliable passive-aggressive tactics failed. She attracted a lot of attention at Midway airport as they boarded the plane in handcuffs. Although Flo was a fight-or-flight-risk, the cuffs came off for the trip due to airline regulations. She was on her best behavior this time, resigned to her fate.

Once back in Florida, the immediate plan was to ship her off to Raiford State Penitentiary within 48 hours of her arrival at the county jail. A freshly scoured maximum-security cell was waiting for my mommy dear. This particular cell was usually reserved to isolate mentally deficient or crazed inmates from the general jail population and as solitary confinement for the rowdy insolent ones. So, clarify something for me - which one of these described my mother?

Now safely corralled back in the County Jail, Ma was on the schedule for transfer to Raiford state prison the next day.

May 30, 1955, the Sarasota Herald-tribune headline read:

Mrs. Baran Taken To Raiford

The local media was on the scene when Sheriff Deputies marched Flo from the Main Street jail to the waiting car. With photographers crowding around her, she tried to cover her face with a sweater. Reporters offered the opinion that Flo seemed slimmer than the 170 pounds she carried before the escape. She also seemed less abrasive than usual, not blasting the photogs with her usual profanity laced comments, but engaging in light-hearted conversation. Once in the car, the shackled Flo tried to hide her face by draping her sweater over her head. One reporter said, *"Hey Florence, you look just like one of those Moslem women"*. Flo responded *"I don't feel so good either"*.

With that, the friendly banter ended. Gentlemen, start your engines! Accompanied by Sheriff Boyer and three manly deputies possessing the requisite upper body strength, handcuffs and side arms, Flo began the 4-hour journey to the state prison located in the northeast corner of Florida. After a few minutes into the trip, they received word that States Attorney Smiley wanted to talk things over with the Flo-meister. The Flo-meister agreed, hoping that there might be a chance at redemption, forgiveness and a big devil's food layer cake with chocolate frosting and two scoops of French vanilla ice cream at the end of the rainbow. They made a detour to the Manatee County Jail in Bradenton where Flo assumed she could relax for a couple of days and enjoy a casual one-on-one chat with Smiley. As one could imagine, Smiley was in no mood to talk about the weather.

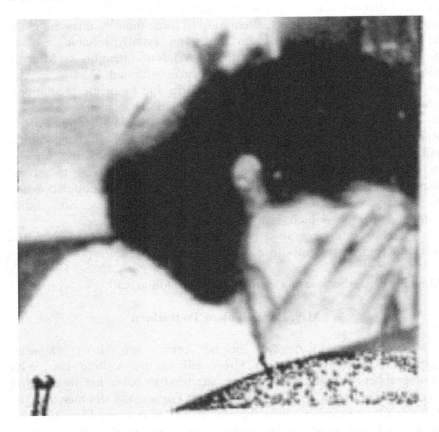

She's finally on her way to the Florida big house.
My momma could run but she couldn't hide.
Courtesy Sarasota Herald-Tribune Copyright 1955

St. Petersburg Times headline of Tuesday, May 31st, 1955 read:

Mrs. Baran Grilled By States Attorney

States Attorney Mack Smiley was tight-lipped with the media when questioned about his discussions with the Baran woman. Speculation ranged from leniency on the escape charge in exchange for her testimony to some unspecified "help" for the now 37-year-old woman. By this time, weary of Flo's verbal and behavioral flatulence, Smiley just prayed for the chance to deliver a good ol' fashioned booty spankin'. Whap! Whap! Whap!

140

The case against Dewey Long rested on two points:

1) The three-foot two-by-four Mrs. Baran used to knock a hole in her cell ceiling. The piece of wood belonged in a basement storage room. Dewey Long had the keys to that room as well as Flo's cell.
2) Long refused to take a lie detector test in Miami after first volunteering to go there for that purpose.

The position of light switches pointed to outside help. It was customary for lights to be off overnight. The Sheriff claimed to have other evidence and witnesses but would not disclose any details.

June 1, 1955, The Sarasota Herald-tribune headline read:

Mrs. Baran Held As Witness

Mack Smiley tells the ravenous reporters, *"I believe she may be a very good witness"* for the prosecution of the alleged accomplice in Flo's big sneak-out. By this time, Mrs. Baran was eager to perform some penance for her misdeeds. Maybe a few mea culpas would curry a modicum of favorable treatment from the prosecuting arm of the state of Florida and her soon-to-be sheltering prison authorities. Who knows, maybe she could get her sentence reduced or possibly even probation instead of doing ten years hard time in the Florida heat and humidity all for a little cooperation in nailing the old guy. It was worth a shot.

It would have been great to be in the room listening to the negotiations between Flo and Smiley. In these days of inexpensive video cameras and infinite-bytes of high-speed digital storage, it would have been de rigueur to record the meeting. I wonder how angry ma could have gotten under those circumstances. Probably not very angry at all. By this time, she was playing it more like a purring pussycat instead of a larcenous lioness. Felonious Flo began to acquiesce to the fact that sunny Florida got it right.

Monday, June 6, 1955, the Sarasota Herald-Tribune headline read:

Criminal Court Opens Today With Full Slate

The trial of Dewey Long began on June 8, 1955. If convicted on the charge of aiding a prisoner's escape, Long faced a maximum sentence of ten long years in the pen which is a really long time for a 53 year-old man. Smiley led the prosecution while Long lawyered-up with two local attorneys, Percy Paderewski and Joseph Kramer. There were

21 witnesses for the prosecution while 20 of Long's close friends, co-workers and relatives huddled together for the defense. The trial was going to last about three days, and was refereed by Judge Lynn Gerald in front of the requisite six-man Florida jury. It's always great to hear charges levied in the glorious technical language of our system of justice. To wit;

Florida Case Law LONG v. STATE, 92 So.2d 259. On January 26, 1955 an information was filed by William M. Smiley, States Attorney of the Twelfth Judicial Circuit of the State of Florida for Sarasota County, prosecuting for the State of Florida in the County of Sarasota, containing allegations "that Dewey Long late of the County and State aforesaid, on the 21st day of January the year of our Lord One Thousand Nine Hundred and Fifty-five, in the county and state aforesaid did unlawfully and feloniously convey into a cell block of the Sarasota County Jail, a place of confinement, an instrument, to-wit: a piece of wood, commonly referred to as a 2 X 4, which was a thing useful to aid a prisoner in making her escape.

As expected, Florence was the chief prosecution witness (*"She'll turn on you"*). In a surprise move, the state subpoenaed Flo's teenage admirer, now 16, from Cincinnati, Ohio to bolster their case against Dewey.

Friday, June 10, 1955, The Sarasota Herald-tribune headline read:

Mrs. Baran Tells How She Escaped

"A telephone trap, a laughing but confused Florence Baran, tales of jailhouse love-making and vigorous and penetrating cross examination kept excitement high in circuit court yesterday as Dewey Long, 53, former courthouse maintenance man went on trial on a charge of aiding in the escape of a prisoner."
Copyright 1955

States Attorney Smiley had first crack at Flo followed by cross examination by defense Attorney Paderewski. The testimony, described as being *"fanciful"* and *"at times humorous"*, was never boring.

FLORENCE IS BACK—Mrs. Florence Baran, who is facing a prison term as an accomplice in a local robbery, is returned to Sarasota to testify in the case against Dewey Long, courthouse maintenance man, who is charged with aiding her escape from the local jail. Deputy Sheriff John Townsend accompanies her to the courtroom. Mrs. Baran, described by Sheriff Ross Boyer as a "tough woman" was arrested by FBI agents in Chicago a few months after her escape.

Courtesy Sarasota Herald-Tribune Copyright 1955

Mrs. Baran relished the opportunity to tell her story. She gleefully reported that Long had been extra friendly toward her since her arrival in the county jail on August 1, 1954. During her five-month stay at Sheriff Boyer's county jail, Flo had plenty of time to hear the details of how another prisoner once made his way to freedom from the same cell. An inmate knocked a hole in the plaster ceiling and made his way through the attic to accomplish that escape. Long insisted that she could do the same anytime she wanted. Dewey went so far as to drive a nail into the ceiling at the exact spot where the ceiling repair had been made inviting Flo to give it a go.

She continued to nail Long when it was revealed that two days before her escape he gave her an eight-inch screwdriver to start the hole and she said he said there was a three foot long 2-by-4 in the attic. The board could be used as a ram to make the hole large enough or as a brace so she could lift herself into the attic.

Mack Smiley asked Flo to tell the men of the jury how she made her way out of the attic. She described how easy it was descending the permanently mounted steel ladder on the wall in the Grand Jury room closet. Once there, she took the stairway down into the vacant 1st floor hallway. The Sheriff's office was at the west wing of the building. Flo was careful to avoid that by exiting the building through the east wing doorway onto Main Street. After reaching the intersection of Main and Washington Street, she hitchhiked a ride from three people in a car. They had been out drinking and were glad to give the damsel in distress some assistance. The gender of the party people in the car was not immediately disclosed. She gladly accepted the invitation to have some beers at their home where she stayed for two days. After that, they took her to a local gas station on US 301 where she begged a ride from a *"salesman from New York who was lost"*. Flo claimed she stayed at a Tampa motel until receiving money from husband Wally in Chicago to purchase a train ticket home. Safely back in Chicago, Flo stayed at home with hubby and the six kids until her arrest three months later by FBI agents.

Some of this testimony, however, was at odds with other known facts stated months earlier but nobody seemed to notice or just declined to object. Aunt Stella actually wired her the money, not Wally. She was protecting her sister no doubt.

Paderewski had little patience with Flo in his cross-examination. He ridiculed Flo's testimony about being picked up by people whose names she could not remember. He suggested she fabricated the whole thing. Later Sheriff Boyer and Smiley produced two witnesses. These were the dudes that picked up Flo that starry night in January. The men, Wallace Whidden and Perry Robert Tate, freely admitted that they picked up the hitchhiking escapee although they were unaware that she had just left the friendly confines of Boyer Bastille. The pair were cruising the streets after drinking and dancing enjoying Sarasota's 1950's nightlife. They bought whatever story she told them and invited her to join them along with their girl friend to continue the late night party. They went to a two-room apartment with a kitchen and one bedroom where they had a few more beers, food and some music. That was 'music' to Flo's ears I'm sure. Yesterday, baloney sandwiches and lukewarm coffee – the next day, beer, home cooked meals and music blaring from something other than a police radio – life is good and getting better. The men were uncertain of or not willing to discuss the sleeping arrangements. After a certain number of beers, many people are uncertain about certain details. In general, they corroborated Florence's story minus/plus a factoid here and there.

Paderewski then reminded Flo that when she was in the guarded grasp of the Federal Bureau of Investigation in Chicago, she admitted making a sworn statement that cleared Long of all guilt in connection with her escape. She explained away that anomaly by stating Dewey didn't physically help her escape. He just provided *"the ways and means"*. Paderewski then persuaded Flo to admit she was in possession of a ball peen hammer in her cell in the weeks before she broke out. When asked why she didn't use it, Flo simply explained she didn't think of it since she already was in possession of the piece of lumber there to enlarge the hole.

The cross-examination revealed another salient point when Flo insisted she never gave or promised Long anything.

Then it was Smiley's turn to score some points for the prosecution. The "Cincinnati Kid" now made his debut on the witness stand. The state was trying to prove that the motive for Dewey's assistance was *"love"* or some other form of amorous "wink-wink" reward. The boy was in the same cellblock as Flo. Recall that he had is own crush on her but that was not brought up in the testimony. The kid stated that he observed *"some lovemaking"* between Flo and Dewey.

"What do you mean by 'lovemaking'?" Mack asked the youth. *"Aw, just petting and kissing"* was the reply.

Defense attorney Kramer then got his chance for cross-examination. The question of the lovemaking was clarified when Kramer asked the kid for more detail. The boy answered *"He never came into the cell"* indicating that they pawed and smooched between the bars. The boy had given a pretrial statement to the lawyers with his father present. The statement was intended to include everything the youth could remember about the case. Kramer reminded the boy that his description of events did not mention anything about jailhouse lovemaking. *"No further questions, your Honor."*

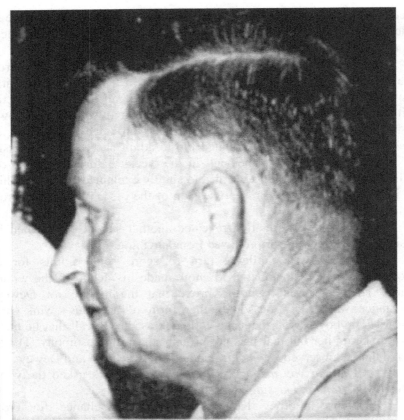

NAMED IN ESCAPE PLOT—Dewey Long, former county courthouse maintenance man, now on trial for aiding Florence Baran escape from her jail cell, is shown in the courthouse at recess yesterday. Mrs. Baran told the court yesterday Long assisted her.

Courtesy Sarasota Herald-Tribune Copyright 1955

As if this trial wasn't fun enough already, another surprising aspect of the case was revealed. Shortly after the escape, the sheriff and State's Attorney resorted to some creative investigative techniques in an attempt to corner Dewey. They were convinced Long was their man so they enlisted the help of employees of the local music radio station WSPB AM. A plot was hatched to enact a fake long distance telephone call from Flo in order to make Dewey say what the authorities wanted to hear - admission of his involvement with Flo while capturing every syllable of the conversation with a tape recorder. Smiley wanted to introduce the tape as evidence.

146

The actors in the ruse were station traffic manager, Miss Jo Ann King performing as Florence, the music librarian Miss Joy Cone, playing a long distance operator and finally David Hale, the station's program director doing the technical work of making the recording. The phony call was directed to the courthouse deputy circuit clerk Robert Getman a few days after Flo "*went that-a-way*".

It was undecided whether to include the tape as evidence. Before the second day of testimony began, Judge Gerald held a briefing in his chambers without the jury present. This meeting included all attorneys, and the actors Cone, King and Hale. The story of the fake phone call needed to be clarified/verified.

Miss Cone said "*Long distance call for Mr. Long*". The deputy clerk hands Long the phone. Miss Cone said "*One moment, long distance is calling.*"

According to Miss King, Flo and Long exchanged greetings. Long then asked the bogus Florence if she had been captured and, if she did, please not mention the two-by-four. The bogus "Florence" answered in the negative and promised not to snitch. This was just the kind of talk the prosecution was hoping for.

Then pretender-Flo, Miss King, asked Dewey to meet her at a local motel to which he replied "*I can't*". Miss King offered the opinion that Long was getting wary and started to hesitate.

Paderewski strongly objected to Miss King's interpretation of Dewey's mood. Miss Cone had also used the same word in describing Dewey during the phone call. Judge Gerald urged the witnesses "*just tell what happened*". Paderewski sought to puncture their story when he drove relentlessly at the fact that Hale, Cone and King held a meeting the Wednesday before the trial to discuss the testimony they were about to give.

Judge Gerald then listened to the recording and offered the opinion that it was nearly unintelligible and that the average witness or juror could not make heads or tails of what was being said. With that opinion, the tape was eliminated as evidence in the trial but all other witnesses and their testimony were good to go.

The trial resumed with the prosecution calling Sheriff Ross E. Boyer to the stand. He described incidents in the investigation of the escape and told of finding the two-by-four on top of one of the cages in the cellblock.

In the subsequent cross-examination, Kramer aggressively pursued certain facts from Boyer, including that Flo had made two previous attempts at escape. In one attempt, she had removed a steel door from its hinges. Kramer then handed the allegedly guilty wooden two-by-four to Boyer and asked him to tell the jury if there was any sign of plaster on the ends. Sheriff admitted that both ends were clean. Boyer stated that all trustees in the jail had occasional freedom from the building. Kramer made much of this fact pointing to the conclusion that any one of them or anyone within the jailhouse could have assisted in the escape - a point well taken. Dewey Long wasn't the only person in the employ of the Sarasota County Courthouse who knew of the escape years earlier.

After the radio station trio of King, Cone and Hale told their story, Dewey took the witness stand. He had to explain away the two-by-four. Did he put it there for Flo or was it just gathering dust up in the attic with other junk? Dewey thought his goose was cooked for mentioning it to the fake Flo on the phone. At the time of the escape, Long was already on a six month probation for his job. This was because of an incident involving hiring of contractors for a small project that he was supposed to take care of personally in addition to some other unspecified dereliction of duty. This was verified by testimony from Sarasota County Commissioner Glenn R. Leach. Spending taxpayer's money when not necessary – a long-standing Chicago tradition not so well received in the sunny Sarasota south – not so well received when you are testifying under oath in front of the media, your wife, your friends, your God and country. Dewey insisted that he just feared for his job. He tried to deflect the accusation of planting the errant piece of wood by telling the faux Flo to hush up about it.

Dewey Long had a long list of friends who lived near him in the neighboring town of Fruitville. Long had lived in the town since 1925 and had a fine reputation with the locals. Many of them sat in the courtroom for the two-day trial and some acted as character witnesses. Thirteen men and women paraded to the witness stand to testify as to Long's good character and reputation. Included were two ministers, two former county commissioners, businessmen and tradesmen. He was a church-going man, a family man and a blue-collar man who led a simple, staid and uncomplicated life – until his life became complicated when the Chi-town homemaker-turned-accomplice invaded his world.

Smiley then cross-examined Long, first demanding to know why Long had previously denied any knowledge of the two-by-four. He replied that he could not recall confirming or denying that. Smiley also sought to establish that Long was having marital difficulties during the time he was allegedly "friendly" with Flo. Long denied this as did Mrs. Long when she took the stand in her husband's defense.

Paderewski, Kramer and Smiley continued to spar back and forth scoring and losing points in the process - the American judicial system at work.

Final prosecution witnesses were Deputy Sheriff's Russell Mize and Lonnie Selph. They both told of finding the screwdriver in the attic. Flo had hidden it in a carton of light bulbs. Mize suggested Long was carrying the screwdriver in a package he saw him carry upstairs in the jail house. It was a common practice for Long and other trusted employees to purchase permitted items and bring them to the inmates. Permitted items generally did not include screwdrivers and ball peen hammers.

Sarasota had two circus acts staying in town at the time.
The famous one depicted here and the other show
at the Sarasota County Courthouse on Main street.
Photograph courtesy of Sarasota County Historical Resources,
Bill Blackstone Photography Collection

Sheriff's deputies Russell Mize (L) and George Spannos
at the ready in case Flo tries to make a break for it again.
Photograph courtesy of Sarasota County Historical Resources,
Bill Blackstone Photography Collection

Saturday, June 11, 1955, The Sarasota Herald-tribune headline read:

Long Found Guilty Of Aiding Escape

"Dewey Long, 53-year-old former courthouse maintenance man,
was found guilty last night to a charge of aiding a prisoner in escaping
from the county jail. The six-man jury returned its verdict in the case at
6:20PM – an hour and 43 minutes after they received the charge from

The verdict came as a surprise. The consensus among attendees of the hearing, was that the state failed to prove its case beyond a reasonable doubt.

Ultimately, all of this gnashing of teeth, clandestine plotting and colorful cross-examinations were for naught as the Florida Supreme Court tossed out the conviction on January 26, 1957.

CONVICTION VOIDED IN SARASOTA ESCAPE

TALLAHASSEE, ๗ — The Florida Supreme Court yesterday threw out the conviction of a former maintenance man at the Sarasota County Jail of smuggling a board into a prisoner to aid a jail break.

Dewey Long had drawn a three-year prison sentence.

The court, in an opinion written by Associate Justice A. J. Lopez of Key West, said the state had failed to prove Long actually had smuggled the board into Florence Baran, awaiting transfer to prison to serve a 10-year sentence for robbery.

The court said there may have been sufficient evidence to convict Long of aiding an escape but he had not been charged with this.

The Baran woman made her escape by punching a hole in the ceiling with a screw driver, then knocking out a hole in the roof with the board.

Florida newspaper column from January 26, 1957.
I found this yellowed clipping at Aunt Stella's house in 2006.
Ma mailed it to her sister Stella from the Florida penitentiary.

151

At the conclusion of Dewey Long's trial, arrangements were made to resume the journey to deliver Florence to her place of confinement in Raiford. My mother checked into the state prison on the morning of June 21, 1955.

THE FAMILY BACK HOME

Let's Review:

1. In November 1953, Flo escaped the confines of domestic shackles and the daily marital turmoil with Walter.

2. In June 1954, she escaped the confines of adulterous turmoil with wild Bill in Miami and returned to Chicago. That was the end of her seven-month "vacation" from Walter and family.

3. On July 26, 1954, she made her second exit from the family when arrested by US Marshals while I watched from the sidelines.

4. On January 23, 1955, Flo made her triumphant return to Chicago after a six month absence when she escaped from Sheriff Boyer's Sarasota County Jail.

5. On April 26, 1955, the feds caught up with her. After 30 days, Sheriff Boyer and his entourage came to Chicago for the second time to bring mommy dear back to Florida.

6. On June 21, 1955, Flo began her ten-year confinement in the sunshine state's big house after testifying for the prosecution in Dewey Long's trial. I turned 5 years old the next day.

During all of those "missing years", what was going on with the six children and their prematurely cotton-haired father in the other big house back in Chicago?

It's Christmas 1953. The six children are; Nancy 15, Jeanne 13, Loretta 11, Freddie 9, Deanna 7 and Larry 3. The father of the house is 43 and the mother is MIA (Missing In Action, Mom Is Absent, Ma Isn't Around, Momma In Absentia, Mother's Inevitable Arrest, etc).

President Eisenhower was finishing his first year in office and the Cold War was gathering momentum. Korean War veterans were coming home. There was a recession in the economy and people were worried about their jobs and the newly minted H-bomb, rumored to be capable of vaporizing small islands during tests in the south Pacific.

Normal everyday Americans were building fallout shelters in their backyard. Shelters were the order of the day on major military installations sanctioned with the survival of western civilization. A few years later, I read a brochure describing the materials of construction and layout of a typical fallout shelter. Start with a big hole in the ground and build a wall with cement blocks. Then put a roof on, run a tube for air and cover it all with dirt. After seeing details of the Hiroshima and Nagasaki holocausts, I was concerned, even at a young age, that the design was not stout enough to withstand half-mile wide atomic fireballs. My thought process was something like *"Shouldn't they be built about a hundred feet underground*?" Luckily, we have never had to go back and examine why so many people suffered instant vaporization in their backyard fallout shelters in major target cities such as Dallas, Miami, Chicago, Boston, and Frostbite Falls Minnesota. The backlog of class-action lawsuits filed against the shelter designers and contractors would be clogging up the courts to this day. Or not. Litigation might be the last thing on the minds of anyone surviving nuclear annihilation.

None of us were very concerned with those worldly distractions when our Christmas tree was glowing with the warmth of the season. We carefully dressed the tree with strings of lights, glass globe ornaments and those ubiquitous plastic Santa's and reindeer. Long ribbons of silver tinsel provided the finishing touch providing that hanging-icicle look. Our hand-made plaster cave with the nativity scene was in its usual place complete with its own blinking light. That light fascinated me for years. How did that thing blink like that? Can you say, "heat activated bimetal switch"? Then there were snowball fights and snowmen in the front yard. We covered the front porch stairs with snow for a makeshift sled hill. The collie dog had a great time running around, barking and squaring off at the humans frolicking in the snow. The absence of the mother of the house tempered the joy and mystery of the holiday season. I was told that ma just left for a vacation. *"Oh. Okay. Fine. Ma will be back soon. Can I have some hot Ovaltine now?"* What did I know? Life goes on. There was a roof over my head and someone made supper. Lassie and I were constant companions. The black cat, Spitfire, purred and kept me warm at night. What could be wrong?

Brother Freddie and the four sisters were all in school, enrolled at St. Thomas the Apostle two short blocks away. Nancy, then a high school sophomore, played her accordion and practiced Liszt on the piano. She was now the Alpha female in the house. She was a tough one and liked to hand out the discipline.

One day she overheard me casually and spontaneously spit out the female dog "B" word. I was on the front porch talking to a friend. Maybe I was trying to be cool. One way to be cool to your friends was to say "bad words". For some reason I said the naughty B word, apparently not in context with a conversation about breeding canines. I doubt that word really made any sense to me. It was just cool man – a bad bad bad bad word!

Nancy came storming out of the house with the screen door slamming behind her and grabbed me by the wrist. She dragged me upstairs to my bedroom. Her hairbrush was to be the instrument used to administer a good lickin' for that verbal atrocity. She tried to turn me over to whack my backside. I squirmed just enough to disrupt her aim. She hit my knee and her brush broke. The bristle end went flying across the room. The brush handle remained in her angry grip. She was horrified at her loss and just let me go. I was lucky. She was a real big girl and I was in for a major ass-whoopin'. Luckily, that plastic hairbrush was no match for my knee.

Christmas dinner, 1953. Nancy snapped this picture being sure to make my head appear attached to the turkey. *Yeah, real funny Nancy.* Ma was probably relaxing in the warm California sun right about then. Jeanne proudly displays her copy of the Carolyn Keene penned Dana Girls mystery story "By the Light of the Study Lamp."
Author's Collection

Loretta (L) and Jeanne enjoy moments together snacking
from a box of chocolates while wrapping presents.
Christmas carols on glorious AM radio helped set the mood.
Author's Collection

I was 3 years old and everyone else seemed much older. Well,
they were. We didn't exactly hang out. Since they were so busy with
their older sibling stuff, they left me alone to watch a lot of TV.

They all had to leave the house during the day for school. Dad
went to work downtown. Who was going to deal with little Larry? The
initial solution was to ship me off to stay with my cousins, the Caliendo
family. Nate Caliendo and my father's younger sister, the other aunt
Helen, lived near 51st and Kildare, a few miles west of us. This worked
out fine for a short time until Scarlet Fever reared its ugly head.
Somehow, I contracted the fever and that ended my vacation with the
cousins. The Caliendos brought me home immediately and I soon
recovered.

Our life long family friends, the Boarmans, lived a half block from us on the 5300 block of S. Kenwood. The mother of the house, Maxine, had recently suffered a mild stroke. She was recovering at home and walking with a cane. Maxine became my second mother during those times. Given the 1950's social climate, it was unusual for a white and black family to be so close. Her six kids were all off to school during the day and she probably enjoyed my company. Nancy would drop me off in the morning along with something for my lunch. It was usually a can of Campbell's Scotch Broth soup. I really liked that tasty version of beef barley soup.

Nancy demonstrates her artistic talent and her
love of horses painting by-the-numbers with water colors.
Author's Collection

In later years, Maxine recalled that I was a very quiet boy. I came with a toy or two and would usually just play on her floor all day. I remember getting sick there once and couldn't make it to the bathroom being too shy to bring up the fact that my food was about to come back up. Yucky stuff splashed onto her dining room floor. Sorry about that, Mrs. Boarman.

Larry is playing with heavy construction equipment that Santa dropped off on his way to Sarasota with a load of harmonicas. I would bring toys like this over to Mrs. Boarman's.
Author's Collection

At home, I would often wake up in the middle of the night and there would be music playing softly in the distance. I would tip-toe down the stairs and stop about halfway to the first floor. Classical music was on dad's radio while he slept in his bed in the dining room. Streetlights served as nightlight to illuminate the scene. It was a peaceful and comforting experience to sit there alone and absorb those midnight symphonies. The serenade would continue until drowsiness would convince me to return to my second floor bed and the purring black cat.

During the summer vacation months, I would just stay home and watch a lot of TV, hang around in the front yard or spend the day playing under the front porch. That was a nice place for a young boy to get lost. I got some toy trucks from Santa and would play with them for hours in the gravel, dirt and spider webs. The Hyde Park Neighborhood Club on Kenwood had programs for youngsters. We would have outings to Washington Park and Jackson Park. Nancy would pack a lunch for me in a brown paper bag, usually a baloney sandwich with an apple or a banana. In later years, with Ma still gone, I was the very definition of a "free range" kid. At 7- or 8-years-old, I would wander solo all over Hyde Park. The University of Chicago campus, Jackson Park and the Museum of Science and Industry were some of my favorite places to explore. These days, it's "helicopter parents" and the DCFS snooping around looking for mothers and fathers to charge with child neglect, abandonment and conduct unbecoming. I have to laugh when I hear of some trivial episode involving a 9-year-old latch-key kid and how the parents are in trouble with the authorities. It's a different world today but I probably did cross paths with a weirdo or two.

Someone mentioned that I used to cry a lot and bang my head against the wall out of frustration or whatever. Maybe I was trying to knock some sense into my head. It sure was a frustrating scene back then but now that I play tennis, I know what *real* frustration is.

Aunt Stella would often come by to check on things. It was a thrill to see her pull up in front of the house in her Army surplus jeep. She said I would run out from under the porch with my dirty face to say hi. She was quite a gal, that Stella; drove a 3 speed stick shift and knew when to shift into 4-wheel drive.

Of course, with Flo gone, Wally could rule the roost with minimal opposition. He stressed the health food angle and pretty much got to play dictator in his own castle. We all had no choice but to go along with the program or fake it with bad acting, sneakiness and avoidance behavior.

Here I am in 1954 just down the street from the Boarman's.
The camera is pointing north on Kenwood toward 54th street.
Nice wagon, huh? And check out those shiny new cars.
The buildings in the background are all gone replaced by
Nichols Park. I am wearing my favorite flannel pajama top.
I wish I had that wagon. Probably a collector's item by now.
Author's Collection

Wally found another health food guru to follow around. Dale Alexander, known as The Codfather, stirred my father's imagination with his claims for better living through bad tasting fish oil. He was an American with no medical credentials, who wrote a book promoting what many viewed as a wildly absurd method of curing arthritis. He recommended taking a daily dose of cod-liver oil on the grounds that it would lubricate the joints from within. Dad would often share his new obsession with us regularly. Yum! Mint flavored cod liver oil. Nice try. This was easy to burp-up too. So that's why the neighbors stopped inviting me over. I smelled like rotting fish!

Aunt Stella with a summer friend. The vacant land behind her would soon become the location of the Philip Murray Grammar School
Author's Collection

One day, when I was 6 or 7, dad left 28 cents for one of my siblings to buy carrots at the National Tea food store on 53rd street. For some reason, that sibling, (who will go unnamed), stole the money and claimed it had disappeared. Dad zeroed in on me for the heinous crime. So, I was on the receiving end of a black leather strap across my little white booty. The ass-whipping ended with the issue unresolved as best as I can remember. But, I did what any self-respecting little boy would do when falsely accused and punished for a "major" crime. The next day, I made a peanut butter sandwich on whole wheat bread and wrapped it in waxed paper. That delicacy, along with a bruised banana, fit into a brown paper bag. I said goodbye to Lassie and ran away from home.

On that warm summer day, I found my way to Lake Michigan south of the 57th Street beach. There was an old breakwater made up of huge granite blocks. The locals used it as a convenient spot for wetting a line to catch perch and whatever other entree' that was swimming around. Little Larry walked out there and marveled at the people with fishing poles and buckets of bait. I was really excited to be there alone.

The footing was somewhat precarious. Those granite blocks were not positioned with any precision - it seems like they were just

161

dumped off a barge in a line stretching about 200 feet into the water. There were gaps where the waves would slosh up and spray you if you were not paying attention. Anyway, I got hungry and sat down to eat my sandwich, saving the banana for later. I had a nice conversation with a friendly black man about fishing and worms. It was warm and I felt a nap coming on. There was a comfortable-looking crevice in the granite where I tried to snooze. The white noise sound of the crashing waves and distant conversations were very comforting.

The next thing I saw was a Chicago cop standing over me asking what I was doing there. Whatever I said was not coherent enough to explain why a youngster was bedding down solo in between some big rocks. OK, the gig was up. The officer took my hand and led me to what might have been a Coast Guard station nearby. This was the cold-war era. The Coast Guard, Army and Navy made their presence known in the Chicago area along with a few Nike missile launch sites scattered up and down the Lake Michigan shoreline. Soon, sister Nancy and the fearsome dictator showed up to take me home.

I had been missing for several hours. I think dad was surprised at me for taking off. Some thirty-odd years later, he apologized for blaming me for that theft. It bothered him all those years. A mystery sibling had admitted doing the deed. Gee! Vindicated at last! Now I can sleep at peace with the assurance that I will never again be falsely fingered or mistakenly maligned for any transgression against person or property for as long as I shall traverse the high plains, graceful valleys and friendly skies of our spinning blue globe. I must admit, to this day, I harbor a nagging and annoying uneasiness about being falsely fingered or mistakenly maligned.

Through the years, all six of us smiling siblings attended venerable St. Thomas the Apostle Grammar School. We shared that distinction with media luminaries Greg and Bryant Gumbel, Mike Veeck, son of White Sox owner Bill Veeck and the legendary comedian and first Tonight Show host, Steve Allen.

The four Baran girls graduated from the all-girl STA high school between 1956 and 1964. You have to give Wally credit for keeping things under control during those "missing years". If the turmoil was not such a disruptive influence, we probably would have been an academically high performing group of jealous siblings. Overall, in spite of the splintered family structure, we all did fine. Everyone took care of themselves. The only real glitch was when brother Fred failed 3rd grade. Given the big mess at home at the time, this was not a big surprise. He had a stuttering issue which caused him some embarrassment and frustration. Thankfully, this was resolved early on and never resurfaced.

Freddie poses while Lassie battles some annoying fleas.
Nice bowtie there Fred. Wasn't that bowtie on sale
for 28 cents at the Woolworth's store on 53rd street?
Author's Collection

Dad and son Fred compete in a scintillating game of checkers.
That game was the only game my father ever really enjoyed.
In later years, Fred became quite good at chess.
Author's Collection

Two of my sisters chimed in recently on how they perceived their mother during their youth. I was young and pretty much oblivious to my abnormal and semi-tumultuous surroundings. I asked them for their memories of the years before I was born and the woman summed up by Sheriff Boyer with the statement *"She's mean. She's tough. She's gonna hurt somebody bad."* Was the sheriff talking about *my* mother? All I remembered about her back then was her homemade chocolate chip cookies loaded with walnuts.

Email From Jeanne:

"Hi Larry, Good question. I have memories of Mom and do wonder what thoughts you, Deanna, and Lori have. What I say is from early experiences: Mom was competitive by voice and behavior. Mom was aggressive and rough, not motherly. She was a real Aries Fire Horse in astrology terminology.

She was a good cook, and I learned how easy it is to make turkey and stuffing. She also let me take out the insides of chickens, and showed me how to cut open and clean out the gizzard, making sure to remove the grit and yellow lining. She would show me the beginnings of the egg inside the chicken, looking like tiny egg yolks.

(Note: about living on 21st place in the early 1940's) *3 kids living in the cold water flat with the coal-burning stove for heat was hard on all. I remember rooms were closed off in the winter. I went thru the doors to those cold rooms. I was barefoot, or wearing gym shoes, and wearing only pull-ups and underwear. I was walking so must have been around 2 years old. Seems like the rooms were empty, or barely furnished. I was a child who lived in an inner world of a trance and only opened to the real world sometimes. I do not remember Nancy at all. She would be 4 years old then. I remember Lori falling down the long staircase with the trike and damaging her thumb.......They* (Flo and Wally) *burned wood in the stove too. I remember Mom being cold and complaining about it. I remember the coal bucket and shovel and Dad getting out the clinkers from the stove. Mom shivering from cold. Most of the time she was stressed by all the physical work of daily life.*

(In Hyde Park) *5 then 6 kids over time and little money equaled pressure. I remember the fighting around holidays for money to buy gifts. She had no friends that I know about, and family helped by taking us to the Indiana Dunes. She discouraged me from bringing home classmates because Mary Lusignan made loud comments about the place when I did bring her over to Dorchester (Misery Mansion) sometime in 1950. Mom whispered to me not to bring her back. I now think the comments insulted Mom because she was overwhelmed by too much stuff like I am. 7 then 8 people in 2 ½ rooms. I never brought anyone else over again.*

Mom liked to go to the 57th street beach and bring a picnic lunch. Poppy seed buns, butter, lettuce, ham, maybe mustard. I think Nancy helped her. In summer we spent all day at the beach. She taught us to make crafts, especially crepe paper

165

flowers, real works of art. We would sit in the dining room off the kitchen. She was critical. I remember Nancy being a perfectionist and it was hard for her to be criticized. She tried so hard to be perfect. I remember Mom being mean to Freddie as a child, screaming at him, crying his heart out, and bringing him to crying like a lost and abandoned child standing in the living room at Dorchester. That makes me sad and tearful even today. I felt his hurt was so deep that I could not tolerate the feelings and blocked them off. I was good at blocking off the pain. I know now I was feeling the same loss and abandonment as he did. I decided that I would never do that to anyone. Children are captives at the mercy of parents, just as husbands and wives are captive to each other.

I remember saying to Mom (being Polish and hearing a news report), *'Don't you just love your Mother country?' I was just a child asking her mother a question. I blocked her words but the expression on her face was scathing like her words, and shut me up. I felt deeply embarrassed by her response. I don't know if she knew I meant Poland. I was thinking of our nationality. Maybe she wondered if I was on the moon or Mars, asking such a question that had no bearing on the time of day. I was 9 or so. She was a married woman, lots of kids and little money. She was concentrating on mopping the floor, laundry, shopping for dinner. Maybe she received verbal attacks instead of answers when she was a child. Remember her age when she and her sisters were no longer living with Grandma Helen* (in the boarding school). *Thinking of my life, experience is everything. How the world works counts.*

I remember one day Mom came in the back door (at Ridgewood Court) *looking like a million, with a poodle cut hairdo, a red orange dress, hoop earrings, new shoes: Mom looked terrific. From then on, I liked her brunette color hair, red orange color clothing, and hoop earrings. ......*

I think now Mom absorbed the frustrations of her daily hand-to- mouth existence and pressures and took them out on us kids. There was little respite to the daily workload for her. Her relief was the beach, Budweiser and old movies at the local bar on Harper or Kenwood, old movies on TV, singing to the songs on the radio and movie musicals. She wrote poetry and of course, Walk Away Blues.

She let Dad have it too. He had the financial pressure to support the whole shebang. He did a good job. He was the steady anchor of the family and Mom was volatile. He knew how to push her buttons. Then she ran when it became too much and

166

life was passing her by. She was in her 30s. Dad was nearing 50.

Being raised in an institution, Mom had little guidance in how to care for kids or organize. Mom had a learning disability too. Bob (Jeanne's husband) *would say 'here comes old steamboat whistle' because Mom talked in a loud voice, like Grandma Helen. Freddie had the stuttering part and I had the cluttering part, which is the area of physical damage in the brain that shows the symptoms. It was difficult for me to learn. When I told Mom that I had a learning disability and it was passed on cause she and her Mom had one, she blew up and vehemently denied it. But how could she know? She was how she was and that was it. My era, my timeline was so different from hers. I went on to* (Psychiatric Nursing) *school thanks to Dad and a Mental Health Grant from the state of Illinois. And I paid back the loan of the $850 to Dad for the first year of school, and the grant. But I learned a little. Mom was a product of her life experience, her choices, her biology, and her astrology. She was a big strong woman, a fire sign, aggressive, dominant, competitive. I have no childhood memories of Mom being gentle She was a strong worker with the horses and the farm chores. She had amazing artistic ability using macramé, crafts, crewelwork, sewing, stuffed toy making. She was a good cook and made the best raisin pie. Caring for children was not her talent. After her stroke* (in 1994), *Mom did appreciate all our help in taking care of her, each in our own way. I like the picture you found of Mom that you recently emailed. To me it shows a vulnerable and gentle expression on her face. We take the good and learn from the not so good life experiences. We make our own choices in life. For better or for worse. She did."*

Jeanne recalled being frightened by the "commie pinko" threat during what we now call "The McCarthy Era". She shut down and became a recluse. Feeling very isolated from the family, she tried her best to leave the cooking and shopping to everyone else. School was difficult. Home was difficult. She escaped fears and feelings of inferiority by reading books. She tried to blend in at school but felt most comfortable reading in the dim light of the bedroom with its cozy dressing room and its dark closet off to the side. On warmer days she would enjoy Nancy Drew mystery stories on the second floor sun porch although the bright sunlight hurt her eyes. Every solution breeds new problems.

Jeanne borrowed this high school graduation dress
from Alice Boarman, June, 1958. Ma Flo was not available
for the ceremony due to a previous incarceration obligation.
Author's Collection

She recalls experiencing dad's sadness. Late one evening, she
ventured downstairs for a snack. In the dark, she saw dad lying on the
couch in the parlor off the kitchen. She could hear him crying softly.
Something told her to go past and say nothing. She got some food and
hurried back upstairs, afraid to say anything. Even today, the memory
brings her to tears. It was hard on dad but he persisted. At his core he
was strong.

To escape the loneliness, Jeanne started volunteering at the
Miserecordia Home. There she met a handicapped boy named Wayne.
She felt like she had met him before, kindred spirits trapped in
circumstances beyond their control. A wave of sadness washed over her
when she realized she could not help him out of his predicament. She

could only give him a hug and be on her way.

All was not daily pain and suffering for her. Active sports were out of the question due to her poor eyesight. Board games and card games like "Fish" helped her through the days. Checkers was a favorite as well as ping-pong at the Hyde Park Neighborhood Club on Kenwood Avenue. Acting in school plays provided a welcome distraction. There were playful nicknames thrown around the house like "Retsie", short for Loretta. Then the silly rhyming started with brilliantly conceived classics such as Nancy Pancy, Jeannie Weenie, Freddie Peddie, Deanna Banana and Luscious Larry. *Luscious Larry?* I don't recall feeling particularly luscious. I guess that's better than Lewd and Lascivious Larry. Of course, the circumstances at the time could have generated Florence Abhorrence or Oh-No-Flo, but I doubt anyone had the inclination or verbal skills to create such poignantly malignant monikers.

Email From Loretta;

> *"..... I read Jeanne's reply and she has a better memory of the years when we were little than I do. I don't even remember falling down the stairs with a bike and breaking my thumb, but I was told that was what happened to it. It was never set right so it is still very crooked.*
>
> *My first memories are of the misery mansion in Hyde Park (5463 S Dorchester), Peter Rabbit books, and bouncing on a large bed. We would stop when Dad got home from work. I remember a wind-up record player and Al Jolson 33's, and playing 'nurse' with Jeanne. I remember watching TV; cowboys and Indians. Dad would watch boxing and baseball mostly.*
>
> *Mom used to make a salad I really liked with grated carrots and sour cream. I remember when she would come home from the store and I would look to see if she had bought sour cream. Her and I would get into a war of the wills about me eating broccoli made with garlic. I didn't like the taste and would stubbornly refuse to eat it. I remember watching to see if Dad would interfere in 'our war' and he never did. I don't remember eating it.*
>
> *I don't remember feeling like she was there for me. I remember her using the washing machine with a wringer on it in the small bathroom at Misery Mansion. She would do what was expected of her I guess, but she was not very motherly. She never said to tie your shoelaces or to watch where you are going, to be careful, or come in when it got dark. We were pretty much left to 'parent' ourselves. I'm sure being brought up in an orphanage didn't help her develop her mothering instincts. I don't ever*

remember feeling that she was very protective.

When we lived on Ridgewood Ct., I was walking along the fence of the school on Kenwood, and a man stopped his car and called to me. He said he would give me a dollar if I went for a ride with him. I told him my mom was waiting for me on the corner and pointed back towards 54th & Kenwood (there was no one on the corner, but I didn't care) then I turned around and ran! It was very scary. I told Mom about it when I got home, but she acted like she didn't believe me. I was very scared and wanted a hug which I never got of course. I also very badly needed to be validated. In a way she had saved me that day though, because she would tell us about terrible things she read in the newspaper and made me afraid of strange men.

I remember going to the store for her, and then being yelled at when I got back because I didn't get the brand she wanted. Either they were out of it, or I couldn't find it, but that experience really was hard on my self confidence, at a time when I was just learning to think and make decisions. It was always like our feelings didn't matter or worse, didn't exist.....and sadly, most of my experiences with Mom were not positive.

Her and Dad would fight, and I remember thinking that what they were fighting about was not the real issue, but didn't know how to identify the real issue. Looking back...maybe a power struggle?

She seemed depressed a lot, and I have a memory of her sitting at the kitchen table rocking back and forth for long periods of time. She loved to watch 'The Hit Parade' on TV, and would drink a little beer to relax herself sometimes at night. She also loved to listen to country and western music on the radio. She wasn't very happy I guess, and may have felt kind of trapped with 6 kids and no $. I remember going with her at Christmas time to find a Christmas tree, and she would try to bargain down the price.....After she left, I would buy the tree, from $ I got from empty bottles or selling pot holders. Sometimes I ended up with 2 trees tied together.

She did bring some joy into our lives though, with the times at the beach, or at Riverview every summer (after a big fight with Dad to get him to spring for it), buying the 2 collies, Laddie and Lady,

She was a fighter though. I remember when she would argue with Dad, and occasionally throw a loaf of bread at him. She also fought with him about Christmas because he wouldn't give us anything, but his company had given him $ for us. To solve the problem, his boss's wife would buy us all presents at

170

Christmas time - boxed and wrapped. I remember looking forward to him bringing a huge package home at Christmas time...Mom didn't have any money so we all got 1 present. Dad would take me for a walk with him after Christmas to a phone booth so I could thank his boss for the presents."

For better or for worse, Loretta and everyone else just went around fending for themselves. Loretta was often given the task of shopping for lunch meat, ground beef and other groceries after school. Dad liked to dine on the 14-year old's version of beef stew. Loretta's hands got so red from washing her clothes by hand that a nun at school asked her about it. In addition to collecting bottles and selling handmade pot holders door-to-door, the third oldest earned money babysitting so she could buy clothes and makeup. I remember wide-mouthed blue jars of Noxema skin cream scattered around the house.

I give Loretta credit for teaching me how to ride a bike. We borrowed a red 24" bicycle from one of the older Costello boys living nearby. I think his name was John or Barry. The Murray school playground across the street made a perfect place to fall over while trying to stay upright on the two-wheeled vehicle – no training wheels for me. Loretta patiently held the bike while I pedaled. When she let go, gravity would eventually take me down. After a couple days though, I had it nailed. I would constantly beg Costello to use his bike for a few minutes. He was pretty good about sharing it.

Retsie always went to church on Sunday, enjoyed horseback riding at the 59th street Midway stables and just tried to keep things normal. She felt bad about what Ma did but could not totally blame her for running off because she was so unhappy. Then there was the contentious relationship with big sis Nancy. Cat fights with hair pulling and nail scratching broke out from time-to-time. Nancy was in the habit of calling Loretta "double ugly" and other unflattering names. Loretta never could figure out why she was the target of big sister's verbal and physical abuse. Maybe Nancy considered Retsie a personal threat to her dominance because she was such a little cutie or that their dad liked her cooking so much. This constant harassment was the norm until Loretta fought back one day with such feline fury that Nancy never bothered her again. Meanwhile, Freddie and I steered clear of that discord as much as possible.

Loretta (L) and best friend Lynn about 1958.
There was always a collie around.
Author's Collection

Deanna, however, recalls a big sister who was helpful and considerate. Nancy helped her with daily chores and simple things like fixing her hair for school and shopping for clothes. With the mother out of town, Nancy was the sponsor for Deanna's first Communion.

So there you have it, the report from the trenches. Those emails help paint the picture of a woman trapped in a role that was never part of her original dream sequence as a youngster.

Living her formative years in a boarding school, from age 4 thru 15, Flo probably entered marriage with some Hollywood movie fantasy of romance and an ideal family life she never experienced with her parents. She remembered virtually nothing about her father and was deprived of his influence. Now Florence was on a great adventure. With her younger boyfriend, she escaped to search for a real life out on the road while we were holding our own back home.

Perhaps living a "Bogie and Bacall" fantasy, they were touring the Great American Southwest with stops in Oklahoma City; Phoenix, Arizona; Pasadena and Los Angeles, California. Continuing east, they arrived in Florida making stops in Pensacola and Panama City in the Florida panhandle, Bill's old stompin' grounds.

172

Passing through Mobile, Alabama, on US Highway 90, Bill might have reminisced with Flo; *"This is where those 'Bama boys arrested me in 1945 on those trumped up armed robbery charges. Who, me? Do I look like someone who would point a gun at some old lady's wrinkled mug and insist that she 'Give me the money'? That's a bogus charge if I ever heard one."*

With Ma gone, Aunt Stella (in back) would often watch over the family as evidenced by this beach scene from 1954. They put me to work taking the picture with Nancy's camera.
Author's Collection

Agnes Gaskell, Bill's mom, lived a short distance from us. I carry a vague mental image of that 50-something woman closing our front gate one day and walking south on Ridgewood Court. She must have been at the house for conversations with dad. I wonder how she

173

explained away her son's adulterous involvement with my mother. Did she tell Wally about Billy-boy's less than honorable discharge from the Navy? Did she even know about it? What about the Alabama DOC days and first wife, Miss G? I'm guessing that she defended her son at every turn just like many moms would. Those were some perplexing and unsettling times.

Free at last, Ma is on 'vacation' at the Gulf of Mexico.
"Hi kids. I'll be home soon. Promise."
She kept the promise but her return home in 1954 was short-lived.
This is a photo from the album I found at Aunt Stella's in 2006.
Author's Collection

"....a skilled maker of dolls and other toy creatures..."

Florence Gaskell, Prisoner Number 55220

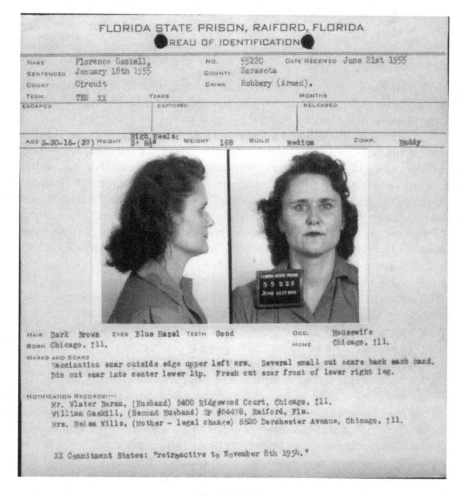

FLORIDA STATE PRISON, RAIFORD, FLORIDA
BUREAU OF IDENTIFICATION

NAME	Florence Gaskell,	NO. 55220	DATE RECEIVED June 21st 1955
SENTENCED	January 18th 1955	COUNTY	Sarasota
COURT	Circuit	CRIME	Robbery (Armed).
TERM	TEN XX YEARS		MONTHS
ESCAPED		CAPTURED	RELEASED

AGE 3-30-18- (37) HEIGHT 5' 6½" High Heels: WEIGHT 168 BUILD Medium COMP. Ruddy

HAIR Dark Brown EYES Blue Hazel TEETH Good OCC. Housewife
BORN Chicago, Ill. HOME Chicago, Ill.

MARKS AND SCARS
Vaccination scar outside edge upper left arm. Several small cut scars back each hand.
Dim cut scar into center lower lip. Fresh cut scar front of lower right leg.

NOTIFICATION RECORDS:---
Mr. Wlater Baran, (Husband) 5400 Ridgewood Court, Chicago, Ill.
William Gaskill, (Second Husband) SP #54478, Raiford, Fla.
Mrs. Helen Wills, (Mother - legal change) 5520 Dorchester Avenue, Chicago, Ill.

XX Commitment States: "retroactive to November 8th 1954."

Author's Collection

Ma reported for "duty" at Raiford State Prison on June 21, 1955. I turned 5 years old on the next day. We can be sure that the Sarasota law enforcement community was glad she was finally tucked away. I wonder if Sheriff Boyer sent her a well-deserved "Happy Incarceration Day" telegram.

The Sarasota Herald Tribune ran a 1955 New Year's Eve feature story entitled;

Best Sarasota Bets For 1956

Grouped with the news that Boston Red Sox slugger Ted Williams will not be reporting for spring training, Flo was given her send-off:

"Florence Baran won't be around to give Sheriff Ross Boyer any more ulcers for the simple reason she has been removed from his area of concern".

Courtesy Sarasota Herald-Tribune Copyright 1955

Boyer's area of concern became much less hectic since the battling-babe was now under physical sedation - barbed wire, large men with weapons and snarling guard dogs took the battle out of the babe.

Raiford Prison had a reputation for being a tough place. At that time, it housed both male and female prisoners. Established in 1913, Florida's largest and oldest correctional institution had an initial population of close to 600. Given the official name of Raiford Penitentiary, the facility was commonly known as the "State Prison Farm". Some inmates were leased to private businesses, a common practice in those days. Other convicts' duties included farming the 18,000-acre prison property, hopefully learning some kind of marketable skill in the process.

The inmates sometimes earned rewards for their labors. This included allowing them to produce their own theatrical productions, and compete in weekly baseball games. However, reports of guards beating up on inmates soured the positive image that the prison authorities were trying to project. The bad press describing brutal treatment of inmates in the lease system would lead its cancellation in 1923.

In general, living conditions in the prison were very poor. The women especially lived in horrid conditions, housed separately from the men in overcrowded, wooden dormitories. Along with kitchen duty and laundry services, a shoe factory provided employment for the imprisoned femme fatales, churning out about 10 pairs of shoes per day.

Race was a major source of conflict in the early years of the Prison Farm. Two-thirds of the male inmates were of color and one-third white. Segregation existed in every aspect of prison life, from working areas to hospitals to bathrooms. Eighty percent of executions at Raiford were of people of color, despite the fact that most of the Florida population was white.

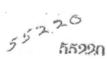

WHITE FEMALE

STATE OF FLORIDA

COMMITMENT TO STATE PRISON

55220

55220

JUN 21 1955

IN THE CIRCUIT COURT

(Court)

IN AND FOR SARASOTA COUNTY, FLORIDA

(County)

FALL Term A. D. 195 4

Date of Conviction 11-8-54 A. D. 195

Date Sentence Passed 1-18-55 A. D. 195

Indictment Bar

Information For

#1050 ROBBERY

STATE OF FLORIDA

vs.

FLORENCE GASKELL, alias FLORENCE BARAN, ETC.,

STATE OF FLORIDA

IN THE NAME AND BY THE AUTHORITY OF THE STATE OF FLORIDA, TO THE SHERIFF OF SAID COUNTY AND THE CUSTODIAN OF THE STATE PRISON, GREETING:

FLORENCE GASKELL, alias FLORENCE BARAN, alias

WHEREAS, FLORENCE WILLS, alias FLORENCE WILSON having been duly

charged by information as above stated and convicted in said

Court for the crime of ROBBERY

and Judgment having been pronounced against her that she be punished by confine-

ment at hard labor in the State Prison for the term of TEN YEARS

all of which appearing to us of record, and a Certified copy of the Judgment being

endorsed hereon and made a part hereof; Now this is to command you, the said Sheriff, to take

FLORENCE GASKELL, alias FLORENCE BARAN, alias FLORENCE WILLS,

and keep and safely deliver the said alias FLORENCE WILSON

into the keeping of the Custodian of the State Prison of the State of Florida forthwith; And this

is to command you, the said Custodian, or other Officer in charge of the State Prison, to receive

FLORENCE GASKELL, alias FLORENCE BARAN, alias FLORENCE WILLS,

of and from the Sheriff of the said County the said alias FLORENCE WILSON

convicted and sentenced as aforesaid, and her the said

FLORENCE GASKELL, alias FLORENCE BARAN, alias FLORENCE

WILLS, alias FLORENCE WILSON keep and imprison in the State

Prison of the State of Florida for the term of TEN YEARS

And these Presents shall be your Authority for the same. Herein fail not.

WITNESS the Honorable W. T. HARRISON

Judge of the CIRCUIT COURT

(Court)

in and for SARASOTA County, Florida

as also W. A. WYNNE Clerk, and the Seal

thereof, this the 18th day of January A. D. 1955

W. A. WYNNE

Clerk of the Court.

By _____

Deputy Clerk

Ma checks into the Raiford hotel the day before my 5th birthday.

Author's Collection

177

Eventually, construction began on a new facility outside Lowell Florida. Now the oldest state facility for women, it opened in April, 1956, as Florida Correctional Institution, housing all custody levels including death row. This was a minimum custody open compound styled facility housing around 300 female inmates. All Raiford women were transferred there when it opened.

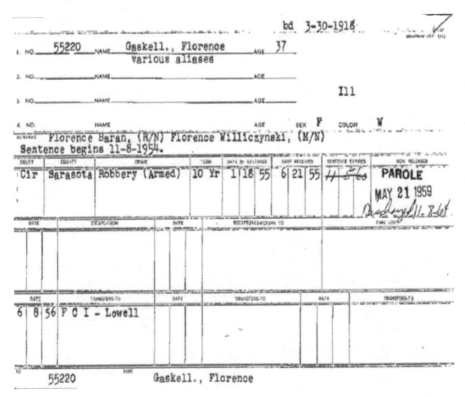

On June 8, 1956, Flo transferred to Lowell Correctional Institution
along with all the other females housed at Raiford.
Author's Collection

Flo was a good prisoner serving out her time at Lowell. Flo learned to crochet creating elaborate doilies and sweaters. She became a skilled maker of dolls and other toy creatures some of which were shipped back home to the family in Chicago. We received sock monkeys, little dogs, cats and a cute blue elephant stuffed with foam cubes. That elephant somehow sprung a leak spewing its multicolored foam innards all over my bedroom. I seem to remember throwing that little pachyderm around bouncing it off the walls, punting it and punching it in the nose (trunk) which probably contributed to the leak. I must have been very frustrated about something that day.

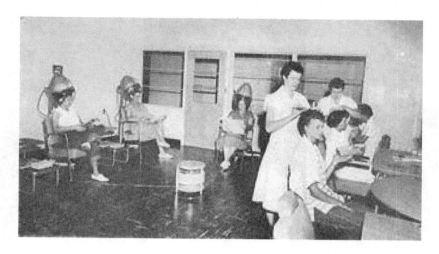

Lowell Correctional Center beauty parlor, 1950's. Just how beautiful does a convicted felon need to be? It's probably my imagination, but the gal wearing the space helmet on the far left looks like mommy.

Courtesy Lowell Correctional Center

I'm visiting the Lowell C.I. entrance March, 2011.

Author's Collection

Convicted graduate Florence Baran (standing in the back row, far left),
earned her high school diploma at Lowell Correctional Institution.
Flo and the eight other naughty girls spent their time wisely
as Jesus monitored the situation from above.
Author's Collection

"Be it known that, one month before her parole........"
My mother is back to using her legal married name instead
of her illegal married name. Good idea ma.
You are coming back home soon.
Author's Collection

The Florida Parole Commission determined that Florence had spent enough time at Lowell. They were convinced prisoner 55220 had displayed a good attitude and stayed out of trouble to avoid solitary confinement and other punishments. She demonstrated a willingness to learn from her mistakes and vowed to stay on the straight and narrow if released back into society. So, Flo goes home in 1959 to begin 5 years of good behavior on probation.

CO #31064

Florida Parole Commission
Tallahassee, Florida

Certificate of Parole

No. 9136

KNOW ALL MEN BY THESE PRESENTS:

Pursuant to thorough investigation and consideration the Florida Parole Commission finds that **Florence Gaskell**_____, Prison No. **55220**_____, is eligible to be placed on parole under Section 12, Chapter 20519, Laws of Florida, Acts of 1941, as amended, and that there is reasonable probability that said prisoner will live and conduct __her__ self as a respectable and law-abiding person, and also that the release of said prisoner will be compatible with __her__ own welfare and the welfare of society, and it appearing further that the Florida Parole Commission is satisfied that said prisoner will be suitably employed in self-sustaining employment, or that __she__ will not become a public charge on release:

It is hereby ordered that said prisoner be, and hereby is, paroled effective **May 21**_____, 19**59**, and that __she__ remain under supervision subject to the specific conditions of parole as listed on the reverse side of this Order until **November 8**_____, 19**64**, unless otherwise released, or until other action may be taken by the Florida Parole Commission.

IN WITNESS WHEREOF this certificate bearing the seal of the Florida Parole Commission is issued this the **5th**_____ day of _____**May**_____, 19**59**.

Florida Parole Commission
BY:

Raymond B. Marsh

Jos. Y. Cheney

Francis R. Bridges, Jr.
Commissioners

The above-named prisoner was released on the **21** day of _____**May**_____, 19**59**

H. B. Wins   Superintendent or Warden

Ma is sent packing May 21, 1959
Author's Collection

182

BUREAU OF IDENTIFICATION
FLORIDA STATE PRISON
RAIFORD, FLORIDA

March 8th 1955

Honorable Nathan Mayo,	Re: William Howard Gaskell,	C&S ME No. **54477**
Commissioner of Agriculture,	Aliases	
Prison Division		
Tallahassee, Florida.		
Dear Sir:	New	
	Old Fla. SP. No's 54478	

Below is a copy of our record on the above-named, now in this Institution.

Crime	Robbery (Armed).
Sentenced	November 24th 1954 Court Circuit Term FIFTEEN YEARS County Sarasota
Received	March 4th 1955 Age 1-12-27(28) Height 5' 9 3/4" Weight 176
Build	Medium Comp. Medium Dark Hair Dark Brown Eyes Dark Brown
Teeth	Fair Occ. Electrician
Born	Chicago, Illinois. Home Chicago, Illinois.
Marks & Scars	Vaccination scar above tattoo of word "STEAMBOAT & Alabama Prison No. 50749" upper left arm. Right index finger amputated just below 2nd joint. Tattoo of "HEART" & words "DEATH BEFOR DISHONOR & MOTHER" upper right arm. Dim cut scar center of forehead.
Notification Records	Mrs. Florence Gaskell, (Wife) Now on Escape from Sarasota County Jail. Mrs. Agnes Gaskell (Mother) 5544 Ingleside Avenue, Chicago, Illinois.
Remarks	New No. 54478 is to run consecutively with this No. 54477.

Yours very truly,

R. P. McLendon, Director

FORM 6-8 IM 2-8-54

One of Bill's three mug shots. This one was taken March 8th, 1955
while Flo was still an escapee from Sarasota.
Author's Collection

183

Let's review.

1. Bill was sentenced to 15 years at Raiford for the Morrison's Cafeteria robbery in Sarasota.

2. He was sentenced to 20 years at Raiford for the Ritz Theater robbery in Panama City and 20 more years at Raiford for the robbery in Tallahassee.

After all this sentencing, Wild Bill served only 9 of the 55 years he was awarded by the fine judicial system of the state of Florida. He must have turned on the charm for the parole board hearings. Come October 22, 1963, a new chapter begins for him.

Well, he wasn't a "violent" offender. The .25 caliber Colt pistol was just a prop to enhance his Rocky Sullivan act. Steamboat never fired a shot. Ultimately, I'm sure he was glad of that. Shooting a civilian on his watch would not have enhanced his chances with the parole board. The south side Chicago bad boy just liked to intimidate his victims in order to harvest legal tender for himself and his lovely Polish paramour. Those were interesting times and fun while it lasted. But, after all this commotion and disruption and fear and anger he caused and time and money squandered, I must ask "*What was he thinking?*" Perhaps he wasn't. Perhaps when a person is "devoid of a moral compass", they might be inclined to make decisions that are not in their best interest or in the best interest of people he befriended over the years. For whatever reason, his total prison sentence(s) was reduced to 14 years. His parole lasted until October 22, 1968. Lucky guy I guess.

CO #30071

Florida Parole Commission
Tallahassee, Florida

Certificate of Parole

No. 14782

KNOW ALL MEN BY THESE PRESENTS:

Pursuant to thorough investigation and consideration the Florida Parole Commission finds that **William (Howard) Gaskill (Cockell)**, Prison No. **54470, B-002651**, is eligible to be placed on parole under Section 12, Chapter 20519, Laws of Florida, Acts of 1941, as amended, and that there is reasonable probability that said prisoner will live and conduct **him** self as a respectable and law-abiding person, and also that the release of said prisoner will be compatible with **his** own welfare and the welfare of society, and it appearing further that the Florida Parole Commission is satisfied that said prisoner will be suitably employed in self-sustaining employment, or that **he** will not become a public charge on rele

It is hereby ordered that said prisoner be, and hereby is, paroled effective **October 22**, 19**63**, and that **he** remain under supervision subject to the specific conditions of parole as listed on the reverse side of this Order until **October 22**, 19**65**, unless otherwise released, or until other action may be taken by the Florida Parole Commission.

IN WITNESS WHEREOF this certificate bearing the seal of the Florida Parole Commission is issued this the **8th** day of **October**, 19**63**.

Florida Parole Commission

BY:

Raymond B. Marsh

Francis R. Bridges, Jr.

Commissioners

The above-named prisoner was released on the

22th day of October, 1963.

Superintendent or Warden

RECEIVED

OCT 23 1963

DIVISION OF CORRECTIONS
TALLAHASSEE, FLORIDA

Steamboat sails out of the penitentiary for the final time.
Parole begins on October 22, 1963.
Author's Collection

185

RELEASE TRANSPORTATION

23.05
1-7-23-17-

INMATE REQUEST AND RECEIPT — AUTHORIZATION BY INSTITUTION

-4973

REQUEST BY INMATE FOR TRANSPORTATION UPON DISCHARGE FROM CUSTODY

TO: SUPERINTENDENT OR WARDEN ATTENTION: CLASSIFICATION COMMITTEE	FROM:	INMATE'S NAME GASKELL, William Howard	INMATE'S NO. 54477-WH
TRANSPORTATION REQUESTED:	FROM: Starke, Florida	TO: Cincinnati, Ohio	

I REQUEST THAT UPON MY DISCHARGE FROM CUSTODY OF THE FLORIDA DIVISION OF CORRECTIONS, THAT I BE FURNISHED WITH TRANSPORTATION BETWEEN THE LOCATIONS SHOWN ABOVE. I ACKNOWLEDGE THAT TRANSPORTATION TO BE FURNISHED ME BY THE STATE OF FLORIDA WILL BE SOLELY FOR MY CONVENIENCE AND I WILL NOT NEGOTIATE THE TICKET IN ANY MANNER EXCEPT TO THE DESIGNATED COMMON CARRIER FOR MY PERSONAL TRANSPORTATION. I FURTHER ACKNOWLEDGE THAT, UNTIL SUCH TIME AS I USE THE TICKET, IT WILL REMAIN THE PROPERTY OF THE STATE OF FLORIDA. IN THE EVENT I DO NOT USE THE TICKET OR A PORTION THEREOF, I WILL RETURN IT TO THE INSTITUTION FROM WHICH DISCHARGED OR TO THE FLORIDA DIVISION OF CORRECTIONS, ROOM 543, DOYLE E. CARLTON BUILDING, TALLAHASSEE, FLORIDA.

INMATE'S SIGNATURE: William Howard Gaskell	INMATE'S NUMBER: 54478	DATE: October 22 1963

AUTHORIZATION BY INSTITUTION

NAME OF INSTITUTION: Florida State Prison, Raiford, Florida

CLASSIFICATION COMMITTEE RECOMMENDATION	APPROVAL AS REQUESTED BY INMATE	X	DISAPPROVAL (SEE COMMENTS BELOW)
	OTHER RECOMMENDATIONS AND COMMENTS:		

SIGNATURE:	TITLE: Correctional Off II	DATE: October 22 1963

APPROVED FOR INSTITUTION	X	APPROVED — COMPLIES WITH STATUTES OF STATE OF FLORIDA AND RULES AND REGULATIONS OF BOARD OF COMMISSIONERS OF STATE INSTITUTIONS AND DIVISION OF CORRECTIONS.
		DISAPPROVED

SIGNATURE:	TITLE: Superintendent	DATE: October 22 1963

INMATE'S RECEIPT FOR TICKET

CARRIER: SOUTHERN GREYHOUND LINES	TICKET FORM NO. A-2	TICKET NUMBER: 221236
TRANSPORTATION: FROM: Starke, Florida	TO: Cincinnati, Ohio	TPO NO. 450-2

I HEREBY ACKNOWLEDGE RECEIPT OF THE ABOVE DESCRIBED TICKET:	SIGNATURE OF DISCHARGEE: William Howard Gaskell
DATE: PAROLE October 22 19 63	SIGNATURE OF WITNESS:

DISTRIBUTION

ORIGINAL — CENTRAL OFFICE
SECOND COPY — INMATE FILE JACKET — INSTITUTION

Good behavior in the slammer earns Bill Gaskell a Greyhound bus ticket from Starks, Florida, to Cincinnati, Ohio, October 22, 1963
Author's Collection

One question remains; why did Bill go to Cincinnati, Ohio, upon his release? The record shows he was to report to his parole officer downtown in Chicago every month. Did he keep in touch with the Ohio youth who had the crush on Flo? Perhaps he knew of the John Kile family his parents stayed with briefly in 1920 in nearby Canton. I guess we'll never know that answer unless someone who reads this knows something about it and posts it on social media for the entire world to see.

Florence Baran on Parole and Beyond

May 23, 1959, was a cool cloudy rainy day on the south side of Chicago. My dad and several of us kids jumped into a taxi and headed to the Illinois Central station on 63rd street. According to the 1959 IC schedule, the train from Florida would arrive at 10:30 AM. No one can recall exactly who all went to meet ma but I guess that doesn't matter now. She was on her way home.

When we arrived at the station, I ran up the wet stairs and sprinted toward the approaching train. My feet went out from under me and I slid across the wet platform. After feeling stupid for a few seconds, I got up, wiped myself off and walked the rest of the way. It was exciting to be there. Ma stepped off the train and walked toward us with a big smile on her face. I hadn't seen her in four years but she looked pretty familiar to this 8 year old. We took hugs all around. The Housewife has landed.

The 63rd Street Illinois Central station where Flo arrived
on The City Of Miami 10:30 AM, May 23, 1959.
Courtesy Special Collections Research Center, University of Chicago Library

Every month, Mrs. Baran had to report to her parole officer, Mr. J. G. Murphy at 160 N. LaSalle Street in downtown Chicago. Ma told me about parole – freedom with restrictions. She had to get approval for any trips she planned to take anywhere outside of Cook County. Flo was on a short leash. Of course, this time she did not have to worry about the FBI snatching her off the streets. Two raucous meetings trading punches and kicks with law enforcement officials was enough excitement for two lifetimes. She was tired of fighting. It was time to settle in, try to be normal and just be home.

As long as I can remember, my father slept in a single bed tucked away in the back corner of the first floor dining room. He had a nightstand with a dark brown bakelite Zenith radio and a gooseneck-reading lamp with a metal shade that burned your fingers if you weren't careful. The rest of the family slept in the four bedrooms on the second floor. My brother had a room all to himself. Spitfire the cat sometimes used the area under his bed for his personal cat box. Yes, we found kitty-turds hiding under Fred's bed. Is this too much information?

Sisters Jeanne and Loretta took the front bedroom just off the sun porch. I shared a bedroom with Deanna for a while. We had a bunk bed there. I had the lower, lucky me! Ma and the oldest, Nancy, shared the middle bedroom. When ma left, I took her bed and when Nancy went off to college, Spitfire and I had the room all to ourselves. With ma's return, we shared that room while dad stayed put in the dining room. Their relationship was still similar to placing a couple of South Pole magnets against each other – invisible irresistible forces driving them apart.

Now that Florence was back, living with Walter was not easy. For Walter, living with Florence was not easy. There was a constant pervasive air of tension in the house with occasional sniping over minutia. After all the discord and separation, those two didn't exactly kiss and make up. To their credit, they tried to live together as best as a wild cat and a mean dog could. It did not always show but they were trying to make things work for the family.

Not a whole lot had changed between husband and wife since November, 1953, except now, ma was an ex-con, convicted felon, on parole. Dad let ma return home in spite of the unanimous objections from his siblings and cousins. He was an independent thinker and figured it was no business of theirs. You can't please everyone so you have to please yourself. Wally was the one trying to raise six beautiful, talented, intelligent, creative, obedient (?), studious (??), sensitive, exceptional kids alone, a daunting task even for two parents. Arriving in late May '59, ma had just missed Jeanne's 19th birthday, celebrated my 9th in June, Loretta's 17th in July, Freddie's 15th in September; November brought Wally's 49th and Deanna's 13th with Nancy's 21st in December.

Ma had lot of catching-up to do – she had to make up for three sudden exits and the long absence.

It was a great day on Thursday, October 1, 1959. Good-God-y'all - the Chicago White Sox were playing the Los Angeles Dodgers in the 1959 World Series. Ma was home to watch it with me on TV in glorious black-and-white. We always seemed to have a Zenith TV in the house.

Since we were south-siders, the Sox were THE team. They had the Sox immortals Nellie Fox, Sherm Lollar, little Luis Aparicio, Jim Landis, Minnie Minoso, Billy Pierce and manager Al Lopez. Let's not forget big Ted Kluszewski (Klu) of the bare biceps and towering home runs. The excitement was high especially when "Hizzonor", Mayor Richard J. Daley ordered the air raid sirens to wail away on the day his Sox won the pennant, a move that initially scared the bejesus out of the cold-war weary populace. Jittery citizens called police and fire departments all over the city. Da Mayor lived just a few blocks from Comiskey Park in the Bridgeport neighborhood and made sure everyone in Chicago knew which team he was rooting for.

The series opened at the old Sox Park, 35th and Shields. Klu had a two-homer, 5-RBI showing in game 1, leading them to an 11-0 demolition of the Walter Alston-led Dodgers. Looking back, the Chicago-area native recalled that first game. It was his biggest thrill in baseball being the first Series game he had ever been in. He ran out onto the field and suddenly realized that this was the only game in the country and millions of people are watching. He got a huge thrill out of it.

I was a big fan of Big Ted who was famous for cutting off the sleeves of his uniform to give his arms extra room. He explained that the sleeves were restricting him from swinging. They could never make a uniform for him that had enough room for his bulging Polish biceps. The newer double-knits give a little. But the old flannel ones didn't. His arms got hung up. So he asked them to shorten the sleeves on his uniforms, but they gave him a lot of flak. One day, he just took a pair of scissors and cut them off.

The Dodgers were also loaded with talent that year. It's no surprise they made it to the big dance with names like Duke Snider, Sandy Koufax, Don Drysdale, Johnny Roseboro, Gil Hodges, Carl Furillo, Wally Moon, Tommy Davis and Don Zimmer; a bunch of Hall-of-Famers. Imagine how great these guys would have been if they had the "juice" afforded to the likes of Mr. McGuire, Mr. Bonds and Mr. Sosa, et al.

The only thing players had back then was Performance Enhancement Dinner - hot dogs, Budweiser and a junkyard dog attitude. Viva La Vida Loca!

While watching that first game, we saw big Klu hit one of his towering homers. With the Comiskey Park crowd cheering in the background, I spontaneously gave ma a kiss on the cheek at that gilded moment. Her reaction to the kiss was unforgettably muted, almost unwanted. She was obviously very uncomfortable with my little smooch. Now that I have had many years to think about it, I suspect she may have felt undeserving of affection due to her guilt for leaving us (me) for that adventurous little foray into the dark side of society. On the other hand, due to her upbringing, natural easy affection may have been foreign to her. On some level though, she was always a semi-stranger to me. I never recall hearing the phrase "I love you" in the family. She left us before we really had a relationship together that I could remember in any detail. My sudden show of affection was probably instinctual. Oh, yeah, and the Sox lost the series 4 games to 2. Nuts! The next year, ma and I ran into Nellie Fox at the Hyde Park shopping center. She told me to go get his autograph. There was no way I had the courage to approach a big star like that. Ma got the autograph – she was not one to shy away from celebrity.

It was June, 1960, and time was marching on. Ma had missed Nancy's high school graduation, Jeanne's grammar school and high school graduations, Loretta's grammar school graduation and Freddie's grammar school graduation.

Nancy was now 21, and ma was going to attend a family graduation for the first time. Big sister earned a teaching degree from what was then known as Rosary College in River Forest, Illinois. That same June, Loretta, 18, graduated from St. Thomas The Apostle High School and Deanna graduated from St Thomas The Apostle grammar school.

Jeanne, now 20, was a sophomore at Loyola University seeking a psychiatric nursing degree. That seems appropriate given the unconventional upbringing she survived. She wanted to understand what-the-hell happened to us in the 1950's. I was still plugging away at the education process carrying on the tradition of under-achievement rampant in our family. Since the runaway mom had paid her debt to society, we lived some semblance of a normal life at the green trimmed, white stucco corner house.

Of course, how can one calculate a mother's remorse for abandoning her brood for a felonious fling? One innocuous incident is seared into my memory. Until recently, this scene laid dormant with no context. On Palm Sunday, 1960, ma was walking home alone from services at St. Thomas the Apostle church. I watched her through a window on the north side of the house. She carried a handful of palms in her right hand while looking down at the ground with what seemed to be great sadness. At the time, I did not process that visual as anything important. However, the chemistry set between our ears has a way of

190

storing information that is miraculous to say the least. Now, more than 50 years later, I can make an informed guess at what she was thinking at that moment. Deep regret? Monumental guilt? Yeah, probably. As the years passed, Ma certainly showed she cared for us all. She was generous with her time and money and really tried to make amends in her own way.

Just before St Patrick's Day in 1961, our collie Lassie became very ill. I came home from school to find her lying on the floor bloated and lethargic. I positioned myself on the floor next to her and draped my right arm over her enlarged belly. In my youthful ignorance, I thought she might be having pups. I was trying to comfort her when ma came home from an errand. She knew immediately that the dog was in serious trouble. She shrieked a command for assistance. Luckily, 17 year-old Freddie was right there. He picked up Lassie, carried her out to his car, eased her into the back seat and sped off with ma to a nearby veterinarian. I was impressed that Fred was able to lift Lassie and handle her almost effortlessly. The next day when I got home from school, I phoned the vet for an update on her condition. He told me it was not good. It was ptomaine poisoning. I had no idea what that meant but it sounded ominous. How did that happen?

My sisters suspected that Walter poisoned the dog. This was either to spite Florence or done for the practical matter of having to vacate our house. We had to leave because of the urban renewal forced upon the residents of Hyde Park by the Rockefeller-funded University of Chicago. We had to move by April '61 and the dog was going to be a 'problem'.

I found out later that Ptomaine poisoning is an outdated term for food poisoning. It arises from the concept that ptomaines, small broken-down proteins in food, were the reason people got sick from food. These days, ptomaine poisoning is actually poisoning by foods that have become infected with different types of bacteria. Food left out, like chicken or tuna salad, can readily develop dangerous bacteria.

So, did Lassie lap up some room-temperature chicken salad? Dogs can eat a lot of vile yummy stuff and still go prancing around looking for more vile yummy stuff without any sign of distress. I had always suspected a neighbor of giving her something. She was an unstoppable barker of a watch-dog, relentlessly challenging people, their pets and pedestrians along the corner-lot-white picket fence stretching from 54th Street and turning south onto Ridgewood Court. I thought that maybe that McCarthy girl gave Lassie her last treat.

Lassie shows off her form in the Murray School
yard across the street from our house.
Author's Collection

My sisters (and Ma) must have had a golden reason to suspect Walter of doing the deed. The girls talked among themselves. What did I know? I was given the "mushroom" treatment (kept in the dark and fed 'fertilizer'). So, Lassie died and this 10 year-old got to learn a new word: *cremation*. We kept her ashes in a brown-glass jar. I dug though the ashes once and saw a canine tooth. RIP good girl. That jar disappeared years later.

In April 1961, we moved into a third floor apartment at 5343 S Harper. It had three bedrooms two baths and a nice balcony. I had to share the bedroom with ma and pa. It was strange to see them sleeping together in the same room.

Black cat Spitfire moved with us. The cat was confused about the new living arrangements. We let her out on the first night there and that was that. Spitfire never returned. I wandered around looking for kitty over the next few days. First Lassie is gone and then Spitfire – very disappointing.

Ricky and Cathy O'Hara lived in the second floor apartment directly below us. The brother and sister were my age and we became friends. Their mom was cool because she had a powder-blue 1960 Ford

Thunderbird. I was visiting them one day when Wally and Flo began one of their shrieking matches that reverberated from upstairs. I felt pretty stupid about that.

Ma managed to get a part time job at a Dutch Mill candy store a half a block away on the busy NE corner of 53rd Street and Harper.

Some sage philosopher once uttered the phrase "It's a small world". Well wuddaya know. At some point, Bill Gaskell's mother moved right around the corner from the Dutch Mill candy store. She rented an apartment at 5230 S Lake Park. What, was she following us? Bad boy Bill was still under wraps at Raiford prison at this time. Now what are the chances that Agnes would get a sweet tooth and decide to visit the local sugar shack for some candy-coated almonds and a nice box of chocolates?

One day there was a huge knock down drag-em-out fight between Flo and Wally. I was hiding in the bedroom while the verbal salvos flew. Flo threw a chair at Wally and hit him. ("She'll turn on you"). I remember him being in tears over that battle. I must speculate that Agnes satiated the aforementioned sweet tooth as a startled Flo waited on a startled Agnes. The word "uncomfortable" comes to mind. I must also entertain the notion that dear old ma told dear old dad about the familiar female customer who needed a sugar fix. Bad idea! Armageddon on Harper.

The Six Kids Grow Up

Fred Baran was older than me by six years. We really didn't hang out. He had his friends and interests but we got along OK. Once when a "friend" of mine was harassing me, Fred set him straight with a big right cross that bloodied the guy's lip. He was a good big brother. At least, he watched out for me.

Fred was always gone hanging out with his friends. They had this "social club" called the "Harper Court Surfs" or just plain "Surfs". Were they a "gang"? I don't know. There was a water tower atop the YMCA on 53rd Street. Before we moved from Ridgewood, I could see that structure from my bedroom. One day, the word "*SURFS*" appeared there in large white block letters. Now how did that get there?

Big brother always seemed to have a cool car. The first one was a black and white 1956 Ford Victoria. Then he bought another '56 Ford, orange and white and primer grey, with a 312 police interceptor engine, and no grill. It was fast and he drove it fast. After we moved to the northwest side Logan Square neighborhood, he got a '64 Thunderbird, which was his pride and joy - oooh, electric windows!

Ma worked at this Dutch Mill Candy store on the ground floor
of this grand old building at the NE corner 53rd and Harper.
Courtesy Special Collections Research Center, University of Chicago Library

He left Chicago Vocational High School early but made up for
that by entering the machinist apprentice program at Western Electric in
Cicero. He graduated, got his certificate and appeared to be on his way to
an interesting and productive career. August 24th, 1971, was a dark day
for our friends and family. He had been suffering from some depression
issues during the summer of 1971 but nobody saw *this* coming. He had
been to counseling but, something wasn't right and never got fixed. He
chose to end his life that day. My mother found him bleeding, still alive
and semi-conscious. A single gunshot to the head had done the damage.
He died in the hospital. We never figured out why the handsome young
man left us.

My brother Fred with his buddies in a real cool daddy-o 1962
moment taking a break from hot rodding another Ford.
Fred is second from the left.
Author's Collection

Larry, Lassie and Freddie pose with a pig pink teddy bear
at Christmas time 1960. I should have put on a clean
pair of pants prior to this photo-shoot
Author's Collection

My sisters started getting married off in the early sixties. Nancy was first. In June, 1961, she married 6'7" Don Kurbat – a towering gentle giant – a really nice fellow. I used to ask Don "How is the weather way up there?" My 10-year old mind could not figure out why he didn't think that was funny. They set up housekeeping in Chicago's Jeffrey neighborhood near 72nd and Constance. Nancy began her short-lived teaching career at a local grammar school. She quickly found out what a short-fused and hot temper she had. The little monsters pushed her buttons and she let 'em have it right back. She eventually left the teaching profession and took other jobs that did not include someone else's noisy children such as bank teller.

Fred's Ford Thunderbird with a close friend
acting as a hood ornament.
Author's Collection

      I would ride the Illinois Central electric train to visit her and to baby sit my one-year old niece, Anne. Hubby Don would often join us in a card game called Mille Bornes. I was at their apartment watching TV when Jack Ruby gunned down Lee Harvey Oswald. That was quite a spectacle. Nancy and Don had three children together in the 1960's. Nancy succumbed to cancer in 1989. She had just turned 50.

      In July of 1962, Loretta, 19, got hitched to Chester B. Jordan, a native of the far south suburb Evergreen Park. Following the wedding, they lived in his parent's basement apartment on 115th Street near Talman. On April 15, 1963, twin girls, Debbie and Joanie, entered the family roster. Everyone made a huge fuss over the twins. I have to admit, they amazed me. Lori and Chet had two more children together.

FLORIDA PROBATION AND PAROLE COMMISSION
TALLAHASSEE, FLORIDA

Certificate of Discharge

To Whom It May Concern:

It appearing to the Florida Probation and Parole Commission that:

__Florence Gaskell__ Pr. No. 55220 CO No. 31064

hereinafter referred to as the aforesaid, was on the _____21st_____ *day*

of _____May_____, 19_59_, *paroled,*

It further appearing that the aforesaid has satisfactorily complied with conditions of the Certificate of Parole,

Now, therefore, effective ___November 8, 1964___, *the aforesaid is discharged from parole and extended best wishes for a successful future.*

FLORIDA PROBATION AND PAROLE COMMISSION

Date: _November 18, 1964_   *Cal R Kell*
                               Administrative Assistant

Parole Form 59

Flo gets out from under her parole obligation on November 8, 1964, ten years to the day since her trial and conviction in Sarasota, Florida.
Author's Collection

In August 1963, it was Jeanne's turn. She married Robert "Bob" Meger. He was a jovial fellow with a love of Mopar autos. He tooled around in his dark blue Dodge that he called "Mariah". He raved about that slant six engine.

Bob was an executive with Kemper Insurance. He made mention

of the fact that they were instrumental in the research behind adding the 3rd brake light on motor vehicles. I was impressed. Their first of four sons came along in February, 1965.

In May, 1971, Deanna married her longtime boyfriend, Carlos Chavez. He was a St. Thomas alumni and a good friend of brother Fred from the Hyde Park days with the "Surfs". I eventually married and had one son, Eric Christopher.

My "Hollywood" Marine Days 1968

1968 was a year of exceptional turmoil in these United States. Assassinations of Martin Luther King and Robert Kennedy were big news. Chicago's Democratic National Convention spawned Mayor Daley's famous quote:

> *"The police are not here to create disorder.*
> *They are here to preserve disorder"*

Then there was the Tet offensive in Viet Nam.

After boot camp at the Marine Corps Recruit Depot in San Diego, I fully expected to be shipped off with an M-16 to join in on the war. The Marines had other plans for me. Apparently, I had done exceptionally well on the square-peg-round-hole placement tests. That fine Catholic education at St. Thomas kept me out of the war. I was sent off to radio tech school at MCRD. Electronics in San Diego was much better than the bush in "the Nam".

At reveille, someone in the barracks always had a radio on. The Beatle's song "Lady Madonna" seemed to play over and over and over again. I did not like the song. That was exceptionally annoying to me at the time - especially at 0530 hours. Hell, I wanted to catch a few more Z's. These days, I can at least appreciate the running bass lines performed by Sir Paul McCartney mainly because I don't have to get out of bed at 0530 unless I really want to.

In April 1968, the ground under my feet rumbled, grumbled, shifted and shook. We were enjoying a casual game of 9-ball in the rec room when the billiard balls started moving around. Someone shouted "Hey shitbird, stop shaking the table". Someone else shouted "Earthquake". Answer B was correct. This was my first taste of 4.5 Richter scale seismic activities in southern California. We bolted out of the building onto the 10 acre parade deck. Once outside, we could hear an omnipresent growl from deep in the earth as the palm trees swayed in the distance. Did someone say "aftershocks"? I slept with my clothes on for several days in case I needed to scramble out of a collapsing barracks.

In 1967, I wanted to eat nails for breakfast. What better outfit to
get fresh nails every morning but in the United States Marine Corps.
I served from 31 October 1967 to 1971. Luckily, no Viet Nam for me.
I served my country as a radio technician at Camp Lejeune, N.C.
Author's Collection

I managed to get into a sticky situation on a holiday weekend. In May, four of us Marines decided to go to Disneyland in nearby Anaheim. It was Memorial Day weekend and the weather was spectacular. That's pretty unusual in Southern California. One of our foursome said he was borrowing a car from a friend of his near the base to use on the day trip. Cool! Here comes Private Brian with a beautiful burgundy 1958 four door Chevy. I will protect his identity by not revealing his last name - he was originally from Chicago's north side before his family moved to California. We traveled north admiring the Pacific Ocean and the dramatic coastal scenery. I remember the Classics 4 song "Spooky" playing on radio station XERB, Los Angeles with DJ Wolfman Jack's raspy excitement framing the intro and outro of the latest hits. It was a glorious time for music and started out as a glorious day. We stopped off briefly in Long Beach so Brian could say hi to his parents.

The car had a noisy muffler. We thought it was cool. A Long Beach motorcycle cop thought it was loud. He pulled us over directing us into a fast food restaurant parking lot. There, to our dismay, we found out that Chicago Brian had a bit of Chicago Gaskell in him. He had stolen the car from San Diego. We all gave Brian the "you-son-of-a-bitch" look when the report crackled over the loudspeaker on the police motorcycle, "Dark red 1958 Chevrolet, reported stolen from San Diego". We're not going to Disneyland. We're going to jail.

The Navy Shore Patrol took three of us to the local brig. Brian confessed to the theft when questioned by the civilian authorities, and cleared us of any involvement. The Navy bussed us back to San Diego after two days in a refrigerated brig cell. And yes, they took our belts so we wouldn't hang ourselves. After his conviction for grand theft auto, Brian earned a Bad Conduct Discharge from the Marines followed by time in the civilian jail. I was on guard duty a few days later when Senator Kennedy joined his brother JFK in the after-life. RFK had crossed paths with assassin Sirhan Sirhan - first MLK in April, then RFK. 1968 was a rough year for the famous.

I finished Ground Radio Repair School in December and reported for duty at Camp Lejeune, NC on January 13, 1969. It was there, two years later, where I received news of my brother's passing.

One day I get a letter from home. Ma says, "We bought a farm in Paw Paw Michigan." Moooo? What the heck are they going to do with 120 acres of heavy clay soil farmland? Oh, did I mention that ma had a horse? Since the kids were all out of the house, she apparently needed something else to feed.

The Michigan Farm Days

After my Honorable Discharge in October 1971, I tooled around Chicago for about 6 months. I was not sure what to do with the next 60 or-so years. Mother and father still lived in Chicago. It was suggested I move to the farm and help ma with her horse. Alright, I'll go for that. I'm always up for an adventure. So, in July of 1972, I packed up a guitar and amp into my standard long-haired hippie issue 1966 Volkswagen van and followed ma and her horse to Paw Paw. I stayed in Michigan for two years learning about farm stuff like making a large manure pile out of small manure piles.

Dad thought we could make money breeding and selling beef-on-the-hoof. He purchased 15 Black Angus cows and a very large angry black bull named Big John. Walter was not a hands-on type of guy. He stayed in Chicago and left Flo and me to figure out how to take care of live beef. I was totally out of my element here but it was fun hanging with the heifers and the owls. I quickly learned how very important it was to remain on the non-bull side of the barnyard fence. I functioned mostly as the handyman and laborer. I discovered that it is not possible to drive a 16-penny nail into seasoned oak planks. The house had no inside toilet. It was 1972 and we used a real out-house in winter. Needless to say, I learned plumbing real fast with the help of a kindly old neighbor, Murdon Anthony. I put in a bathroom after a local contractor installed a septic system. We were moving on up at the old farm!

In the middle of all this, I met musicians in Kalamazoo and played guitar in a few rock bands. For me, Michigan was cattle, horses, manure and music. It was fun but a little strange. The winters were tough. Heating a porous 120 year old farmhouse with a 55 gallon drum wood stove was new to me but survivable. After the herd increased to about 25, it became clear that the cattle thing was not going to work out. The cows escaped to the freedom of Michigan highway M-43 more than once. Those half-ton beef burgers ignored the pain of barbs-on-wire and flattened the fence requiring an urgent call to the neighbors to assist in the Waverly Township morning roundup. Soon the Angus went to market, bull and all. Ma could now concentrate on her horse dreams.

In 1974, I moved back to Chicago, got a haircut and went to electrical and electronics schools. The technical field became my career thanks to the kick-start by the Marines and the GI bill paying the tuition.

Ma at Gramma Wills house in Kalamazoo giving an ear
noogie to Gramma's fluff dog. This 1969 picture was taken
almost 10 years to the day after the Housewife's parole.
My sometimes enigmatic Gramma died one year later.
Author's Collection

December 1977 was exceptionally frigid in the Midwest. After a near-fatal bout with a smoky wood stove on a sub-zero night, ma decided to stop spending winters at the farm. The combination of a small wood-burning stove, a porous rickety old un-insulated farm house, 10-degrees below zero temperature and a strong north wind whistling unimpeded across frozen open farm land made for a mind-changing experience for the adventurous 59-year-old. Smoke inhalation and exposure got her two nights in a warm bed with an oxygen mask. Some Chicago friends of mine volunteered to fetch my mother from the Lakeview hospital in Paw Paw. We helped her pack up, find lodging for the race horse, board up the house and move to the relative safety of a warm comfortably cluttered 3rd floor apartment on Barry Avenue in Chicago's Avondale neighborhood.

Flo visiting grandsons Matthew and Eric with mom Nancy, spring 1968
Author's Collection

In order to avoid any more life-threatening events with smoky wood stoves, we would now close down the farm every winter. Ma found a horse farm conveniently located near Benton Harbor to keep the horse until the following spring. She would then move back to Illinois and spend the windy city winters warring with Walter. She always looked forward to the promise of the next spring so she could escape back to the peace and solitude and the Walterlessness of rural Michigan.

Flo and Wally, May, 1971. At least they were smiling.

Author's Collection

Here I am at the Paw Paw farm with brood mare, Run Vicky, March, 1973. Notice the big belly on the horse. Notice the big hair on the tall human. The foal was born on Friday, April 13th, 1973.

Author's Collection

Flo at the farm with yearling Merry Victor in summer, 1974.
At the time, Ma was shopping around for a thoroughbred trainer.
The Housewife was going to the races!
That grand old cathedral-sized barn disintegrated
in the May 13, 1980, tornado.
Author's Collection

MERRY VICTOR

FLORENCE BARAN   OWNER
H. THATER   TRAINER
JERRY STINE   JOCKEY
BALMORAL PARK

6 FURLONGS 1:15:2
$3,500 PURSE

SILKY STEP 2ND
NERVOUS PILLOW 3RD
JULY 22, 1978
LUONGO PHOTO INC. COPYRIGHT

Flo had a nice time with her first victory at Balmoral Park, July 22, 1978.
In the background, my son, Eric, clings to my forehead.
Author's Collection

On May 13, 1980, ma was in Chicago preparing to travel to open up the farm for her annual summer getaway from Walter. There was a severe weather warning for southwest Michigan that day. As advertised, a tornado traveled eastbound on highway M-43 from Glendale to Kalamazoo. The farm is one mile east of Glendale and got slammed hard – a direct hit. The big old barn was turned into a pile of wood and straw. One shed completely disappeared – the chicken house lost a wall – two more sheds were shredded. The farm house lost a few roof shingles and windows. After making piles of firewood out of our out-buildings, that twister criss-crossed the road for 20 miles finally carving a destructive path through downtown Kalamazoo.

I arrived at the farm the next day to survey the situation and it looked like a war zone. The National Guard was already on the scene beginning the big cleanup. I found our John Deere 2010 tractor under the pile of hay, straw and aged oak wood beams and planks that once was a barn. The yellow cab and steering wheel were crushed. There was massive destruction to farms and businesses all the way to Kalamazoo. A local Michigan writer recently penned a book about that stormy day.

The barn and chicken house before the tornado.
The white farmhouse is barely visible.
Author's Collection

We joked that the tornado should have wrecked the house instead. The barn was a century old gem of a building – full of history. The house was essentially solid but needed a lot of work. Luckily, ma decided to postpone her trip. Otherwise, she might have been caught in the big wind and gotten air-mailed to OZ.

The barn and chicken house after the tornado.
At least now we can see the farmhouse which was barely touched.
It suffered only a little wind damage to the roof.
Author's Collection

Living down on the farm during the warm months, she made good use of the skills learned in the boarding school and the Florida penitentiary. Ma spent much of her time making dolls, stuffed animals, crocheted items as well as growing flowers and vegetables. These creations were entered in the Kalamazoo and Allegan County fairs between 1973 and 1993. Her efforts were rewarded with dozens of ribbons and cash prizes. She would recycle horse manure, coffee grounds and garden waste, which went into the world's largest compost pile. The finished compost made a big difference in the garden. Huge sunflowers

210

would get a lot of attention at the fair as well as her tomatoes, pumpkins and squash. Flo would share her bountiful harvest with us each fall when she traveled to Illinois. A bushel of organic tomatoes was always welcome.

She was alone at the farm much of the time. I wonder how much time she spent dreamily reliving her days on the road with the bandit. She did not socialize with the locals. Anytime spent with neighbors was always in the context of horses and gardens. I don't think she was lonely. The isolation was insulation from anyone uncovering her past. If she wanted company, it was a short ride to Kalamazoo to visit Aunt Stella.

Besides the 1200 pound pet horse, Ma kept a dog around named Sheba. That mixed-breed 50-pound nubile puppy factory brought 45 dogs into the world – five litters of 9 – lots of Sheba's descendents in Van Buren County. In later years, a mother raccoon with three babies took up residence in the farmhouse attic. Ma thought it was her motherly mission to feed that free-loading varmint a daily ration of milk and cat food on the front porch. The downside of keeping a wild creature was the stream of urine that would drip through the ceiling from time to time. Mama coon and the babies also piled up solid waste between the attic rafters. At some point, they left on their own leaving behind that certain bouquet emanating from the 2nd floor attic on those hot humid Michigan summer days.

Some of Ma's ribbons from the Allegan and Kalamazoo County fairs.
Author's Collection

Ma at Detroit Race Course in her Dodge pickup about 1982.
The emblem on the door of that rusty 1974 truck was *"Adventurer"*.
That sounds just about right.
Author's Collection

In 1985, Wally and Flo bought a three flat building at 3216 N. Ridgeway in Chicago's Avondale neighborhood. It was a nice idea since they would have rental income from two families to help with the mortgage. They lived on the first floor and leased out the other two apartments.

Wally was a forward thinking guy sometimes. He was interested in new developments that could save him money. He went with hot water solar panels on the building in 1986. The State of Illinois gave him a $4000 rebate for the energy saving investment. That system made his gas bill shrink to almost zero for several months of the year. People's Gas changed his meter twice suspecting it was defective because the summer gas bill was so low.

I paid them a visit on Saturday evening, February 5, 1994. Ma took me aside and whispered that 83-year-old Wally had endured severe chest pains since Friday. I asked him about that and he said it was not too bad and stated that he would exercise on his mini-trampoline until the pain went away. That was his version of physical therapy. Knowing his aversion to doctors, I suggested quite firmly that he see a doctor if things did not improve. Surprisingly, he seemed to agree with me. He was bouncing on his trampoline in the front room by the pale blue light of the television the last time I saw him alive.

The next day, ma called me and said she could not wake up Wally. She had some difficulty explaining what was wrong. I figured dad was dead. I phoned a tenant in the building and asked him to check things out. A call to 9-1-1 followed and that was that. Wally had died in his sleep probably just a few hours after I had left the previous night. While driving to their home, I thought "So this is what it feels like when your father dies."

When I arrived at the house, I felt dad's cold stiff hand. After the paramedics left, we called the neighborhood funeral home to start the embalming/visitation/funeral process. With the body still in the bedroom, I sat with ma at the kitchen table and asked how she felt about the passing of her husband of 56 years. Without looking up from her dinner, she answered *"Relieved"*. Wow. That one word explained everything about her life and marriage to Walter Baran.

We knew that she stayed at the farm during the warm months for all those years in part to get away from dad. Now, with Wally gone, she could live in peace. The war was over. Ma gave up living at the farm and planned on a life alone back in Chicago. I was surprised at this development. In the summer of 1994, she sold her horse and trailer to a Michigan horseman, retrieved important items from the farmhouse and locked it up. That was the last time she ever saw the farm. Since then, 100 acres of the tillable land has been leased to a local farmer.

On September 17, 1994, six months after Wally's death, the widow had a debilitating stroke. A total blockage of her left inner carotid artery literally knocked her off her feet and changed everything. Her independent lifestyle vanished in an instant.

The battling babe had something new to fight. Now she was at a nursing home in Arlington Heights, Illinois. Eleven months of physical and occupational therapy followed. Ma was difficult to deal with but made good progress. In addition to some paralysis, Flo now suffered from a speech impediment known as aphasia. Luckily, daughter Jeanne worked there as a nurse. Jeanne played helicopter daughter, hovering over the situation making sure her mother received proper care.

Dolls and doggies won prizes for Ma at the
Allegan and Kalamazoo County Fairs. They took time out
from their busy schedule to reunite and pose for this picture
Author's Collection

My sister tried hard to ease Flo's anxiety over her predicament. It was a big job to say the least. Ma's frustration led to some fierce temper tantrums but Jeanne applied her calm even temperament to diffuse the situation time and time again.

The Housewife returned home August 4, 1995, and began 11 years of living with full time caregivers. She drove those Polish ladies crazy. The language barrier along with Flo's speech impairment led to many misunderstandings. Flo, while confined in her wheel chair, would often shriek, holler and slap the kitchen table in frustration in an attempt to correct a misdirected request. The quote from Sheriff Boyer back in 1955 was still ringing true; *"She mean and she's tough........."*. She really didn't mean any harm. Flo was very depressed about her situation. It was difficult at times but at least she did not have to stay in a nursing home.

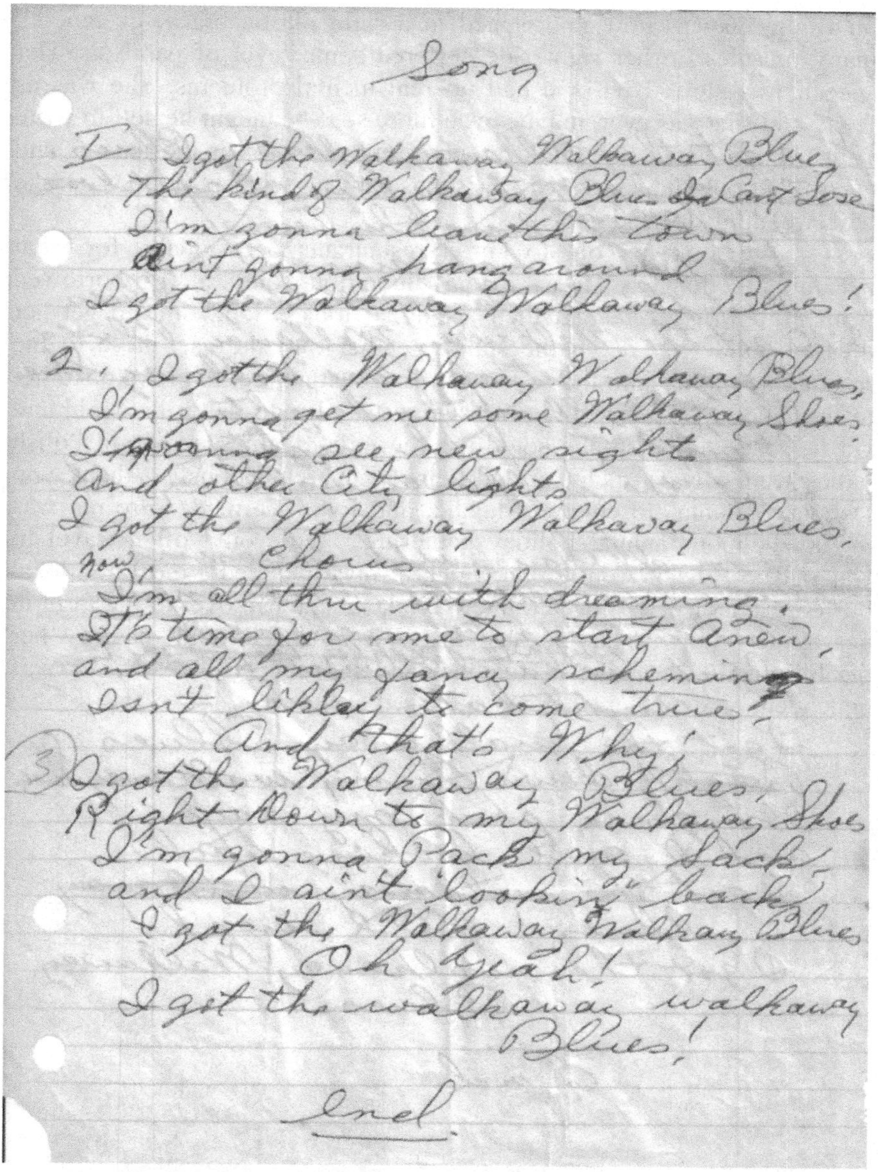

Song

1. I got the Walkaway, Walkaway Blues
The kind of Walkaway Blues I can't lose
I'm gonna leave this town
Aint gonna hang around
I got the Walkaway Walkaway Blues!

2. I got the Walkaway Walkaway Blues,
I'm gonna get me some Walkaway Shoes.
I'm gonna see new sights
And other City lights
I got the Walkaway Walkaway Blues,
now Chorus
I'm all thru with dreaming,
It's time for me to start anew,
and all my fancy scheming,
Isn't likely to come true,
And that's Why,
I got the Walkaway Blues,
Right Down to my Walkaway Shoes
I'm gonna Pack my Sack,
and I ain't looking back,
I got the Walkaway Walkaway Blues
Oh Yeah!
I got the walkaway walkaway
Blues!

End.

The Housewife summarized her life in this simple set of lyrics.
We made a demo recording of The Walkaway Blues in 1985.
Author's Collection

Flo's right arm was totally useless. The arm that once effortlessly guided a speeding getaway car was now limp and flaccid. The hand that could punch and scratch arresting officers now required a sling for support. The right foot that joyfully put-the-pedal-to-the-metal

215

on Route 66 was now imprisoned in a rigid plastic brace. In general, many muscles on her right side suffered some level of paralysis. Her speech was slurred but she had no real mental problems. She was as feisty and sharp as ever, maybe even more so. She taught herself to write with her left hand. She could prepare rent receipts for the tenants and even filled out and addressed Christmas cards. She spent her post-stroke days watching TV and napping.

We took her out to buffet restaurants occasionally for what became affectionately known as the "three hour tour", a term borrowed from the *Gilligan's Island* theme song. It took a long time to get her dressed, guide her down the stairs, get her into the car, drive to the restaurant, get her into the restaurant, find seating, get the food, take her to the toilet, take her to the toilet again, take her to the toilet again and get her back home so she could use the toilet again. Her live-in Polish ladies were always included and helped out tremendously - thank you Danuta, Yolanta, Josephine, Maggie, and Eva. We made sure ma was included in our annual holiday gatherings. We would often travel to Kalamazoo to visit Aunt Stella which always included a meal at a local buffet restaurant. Ma never wanted to take a side trip over to the farm in nearby Paw Paw. That puzzled me. Maybe that would magnify her disability. The farm meant freedom and independence. Now she was dependent on daughters, her son and hired caregivers 24/7.

Jeanne, Flo and Deanna at Aunt Stella's Kalamazoo house in 1998. Notice ma's paralyzed right arm in the sling. Jeanne carried a taser around in case Flo got out of hand. *Oh I'm just kidding*!
Author's Collection

The Ladies Say Goodbye

The Wilczynski sisters passed away in reverse order of the birth. The last born was first to go.

After 80 years of life, Aunt Helen died in her sleep on June 30, 2000. She had an apartment at the Westward Ho retirement community in Phoenix, Arizona. Strange thing but I never met her. She saw me when I was 6 months old but due mostly to geographic circumstances, we never connected. After leaving Kalamazoo in 1957, she lived in Phoenix, then Hollywood for a few years and then back to Phoenix. I had phone conversations with her and we shared letters a few times but that was that. She died without a will, her ex-husband died in the 1980s and her son Lance, a cousin whom I also had never met, died three years before her. Tag! I was it. I served as the executor of her estate. Thankfully, Maricopa County, Arizona, made it relatively easy for me to deal with her affairs.

In October 1999, the two sisters reunite for the last time in Phoenix Arizona. Helen evolved into somewhat of an eccentric. She often wore unusual combinations of clothing, favoring leopard-skin prints and bright red or orange pants-suits
Author's Collection

I flew into the Sky Harbor airport in Phoenix on July 2nd. This was the beginning of a weeklong string of 105-degree days. The desert sun managed to bake an apple I had mistakenly left in my rented car.

Among other tasks, I had to empty Aunt Helen's three-room apartment the best I could. From July 2nd through the 7th, I rummaged through her stuff and finally got to meet her by proxy. There was an almost overwhelming collection of personal items for me to make sense of in one week. She had hundreds and hundreds of pieces of costume jewelry. I mailed about one third of it to my sister Loretta in Colorado. The rest met the dumpster along with the roach infested food from the cabinets, under the bed, behind the couch, in the fridge and, yes, roaches even in the freezer. Helen had collected some nice fashionable clothes over the years. Her next-door neighbor was the happy recipient of a closet full of snazzy garments. Included in the clutter was a huge cache of photographs. It was great to go through several hundred pictures and get to know something about her. She had many professional portraits done when she was in her twenties and chasing her Hollywood dreams. I was finally able to make sense of her life with her husband Ross and their only child, my cousin Lance. Amidst the roaches, stashes of government food items and general clutter, I found a death certificate and other paperwork about the boy. He had been in trouble with the law all his life and met his end in the Maricopa County jail, August of 1997. He was on parole for something, violated that and wound up in the tent city section of the jail. The cause of death was heart failure with hyperthermia as a contributing factor. Being morbidly obese – 400-plus pounds and 5'11" - did not help his situation in the summer heat of the desert southwest. He was 53 years old.

After a series of blood tests to analyze some ominous symptoms, Ma Flo was diagnosed with non-Hodgkin's lymphoma in May of 2005. She was assigned a hospice nurse and lived out her days at home. The Housewife died quietly on Sunday, September 11, 2005. She was given 87 years to complete her life adventure. Jeanne had spent the night with Ma filling in for Jolanta, the Polish caregiver who was on her regular night off. My mother had been, if you will excuse the expression, "circling the drain" lying in bed for two weeks, twitching in a comatose-like state. She had stopped eating weeks earlier and then would not take any fluids. These were signs of the inevitable end of life. That Sunday morning, I was home in Berwyn preparing vegetables, spices and andouille sausage for a tasty batch of jambalaya. When the phone rang at 9 AM, I knew what it was. The preparations for her funeral and burial were all in place. I was able to secure a gravesite right next to Walter at Maryhill Catholic Cemetery in Niles. Some of us shared some dark humor about the placement of her final resting place and its proximity to her departed spouse - the always popular and facetious "*someone is turning over in their grave*" thing. Sorry about that but sometimes you just have to find a molecule of humor when the Grim Reaper shows up to welcome your wayward whimsical mother into the Great Unknown.

In Loving Memory of

Florence M. Baran

Born March 30, 1918
At Rest September 11, 2005

Funeral Services From
Skaja Stanley Funeral Home
Wednesday Sept. 14, 2005 at 10:15 AM

St. Wenceslaus Church
Mass 11:00 AM

Interment
Maryhill Cemetery

MEMORARE

Remember O most gracious Virgin Mary
that never was it known that anyone who
fled to Thy protection, implored Thy help,
and sought Thy intercession was left
unaided. Inspired with this confidence,
I fly unto Thee, O Virgin of virgins, My
Mother! to Thee I come; before Thee I
stand, sinful and sorrowful. Oh Mother of
Word incarnate! despise not my petitions,
but, in Thy mercy, hear and answer me.
-AMEN.

We all have to go sometime
Author's Collection

Aunt Stella savors some cake in celebration of her 90th birthday on March 7, 2006 at the Heritage Hills assisted living center, Kalamazoo. She retired after a 30 year career working for Bronson Hospital in the Central Supply office. She always had such an easy smile.
Author's Collection

Guess where I found the Housewife's gun. Allow me to explain. Around 1947, my Aunt Helen moved to Kalamazoo with her husband Ross. Eventually their marriage went south. The Army veteran was drinking and providing some unnecessary mental cruelty. Helen divorced Ross and bought a house for her and son. It was located at 1424 Olmstead Road right up against the fence at the east side of the Kalamazoo County Fairgrounds. Gramma Wills and Aunt Stella left Chicago together in 1955 and bought the house right next door to Helen. 1420 Olmstead Road is a house nearly identical to Helen's.

They settled in, bringing some of their furniture and belongings from Chicago. Among those belongings was a green can that was once filled with honey. The quart can of honey was probably a freebie from Wally's workplace. When ma returned home after ratting out Bill in Florida, she asked her trusted older sister Stella to hold onto something for her. It was the can, not full of honey this time, but packed with a brown handled .25 caliber Colt semiautomatic pistol, a box of ammo and Gaskell's picture ID badge from US Steel South Works. Flo removed it from the Hyde Park house just before being arrested that hot July day in 1954. Good old Aunt Stella kept that little secret in that little can for more than fifty years.

Let us fast-forward to Kalamazoo, November, 2006. Aunt Stella, 90 years old, was a resident at Heritage Hills Director's Hall. This is the assisted living center at a sprawling retirement community on Portage Road. I had power-of-attorney for Stella's affairs, both property and health care. She trusted me completely. I often traveled from Chicago starting in March 2000 to take care of her issues as they occurred. I made sure her bills were paid, whisked her off to doctor visits and shopped with her at the local Meijer's Thrifty Acres. We usually topped off the visit by stopping for an ice cream cone at the Dairy Queen on Stadium Drive before returning her to Director's Hall.

We often discussed selling her house. She wasn't ready for that. Stella was always holding out hope that she would somehow return to live under her own roof. Until that happened, that little house needed a big clearing out.

Many people have the "clutterbug syndrome", the hoarding habit. Stuff just piles up and never gets thrown out. Uncluttering my aunt's house was a major mini-project. Every time I visited Stella, I would take a side-trip to the house and haul out a few more bulging bags of trash. I was very careful not to toss out anything of value. I employed a triage method in my cleanup. One pile was obvious garbage; another pile was to hold for analysis later; the third pile was important "keeper" stuff. I successfully applied this technique six years earlier at Aunt Helen's Arizona domestic dumpster. Thanks to the three Wilszcynski girls, I was getting lots of practice declutterizing homes.

One cloudy November day, I was at the house for a typical cleanup session. "Where do I start today?" was the question I always asked myself. I decided to tackle the bedroom closet that I had avoided for some time. Several boxes-of-junk, an old vacuum cleaner and piles of debris later, I found the aforementioned green honey can at the bottom of a large box. It was a mind-blowing experience. Five years passed before I figured out the when-how-and-why of that can and its contents.

I never told Aunt Stella of my shocking discovery. On another occasion I had another shocker. I found a photo album full of pictures from the 1950's. It was a collection of Flo and Bill's pics, some of them "Bonnie-and-Clyde-ish". The smiling couple appeared together in photos snapped in Florida and the desert Southwest. I kept a few of them and gave the album to my sister Jeanne. She eventually discarded it. I should have told her to return it to me but too late. Of course, this was three years before I started researching Flo's past. I had no clue that one day I would be scratching and clawing for the tiniest tidbit of information to help solve the mysteries of Ma Flo and her adventures with the bandit.

Aunt Stella's Kalamazoo house in December, 2006.
My mother's gun, ammo and picture album
lay dormant, hidden there for fifty years.
Author's Collection

Aunt Stella was 90 when she passed peacefully in Kalamazoo on December 7, 2006. She was the last of that generation on both sides of my family. Given what I know now, I wish we had talked more. She could have told some very interesting stories about the days of Flo and Bill. My mother's story was not something I ever dwelled upon. I cannot remember any conversation about it with any of my relatives. Then came that day in 2009 when I casually started surfing the internet for Baran-Gaskell. Hot diggity dog, did I hit the jackpot! In the span of six years, I went from knowing zero-point-zilch about our motherly adventurer to becoming the family historian and archivist. Lesson learned. Talk to your elderly relatives about their lives. There's a treasure chest of great stories waiting. You may have seen a TV commercial several years ago for a telephone company. Legendary Alabama football coach, Bear Bryant was the spokesman. He urged us to *"Call your mother. I wish I could"*.

Your author with Maxine Boarman, my "2nd mom" during those strange days while my 1st mom was on vacation in Florida.
Author's Collection

Maxine Boarman acted as my second mother during some of those missing years starting in 1953. She lived out her final days with her daughter Alice in New Jersey. There, I managed to pay her one last visit. Her smile was as big as her heart. We sat for several hours as she told story after story of her life in Chicago, her upbringing in Iowa and her fond remembrances of my sisters hanging out with her daughters. Like Florence, she had six children, three boys and three girls. Their ages closely paralleled our family so it was natural for us to find common ground and friendship which lasts to today. As we talked, I realized I never considered that they were caught up in the racism of the day. They were just our friends and things were normal.

We all had our family tragedies. Like us, they had a mind-wrenching suicide when their youngest son took his own life. Another son was murdered in some love triangle thing. Recently, her son and my good friend Skeeter lost his battle with cancer. As of this writing, both families have three girls remaining. Maxine was as kind-hearted a soul as there ever was.

Bill never got into trouble again. His parole officer was Mr. George Stamper at 160 N. Lasalle Street in Chicago. The Bandit faithfully reported to him without incident for the remainder of his term.

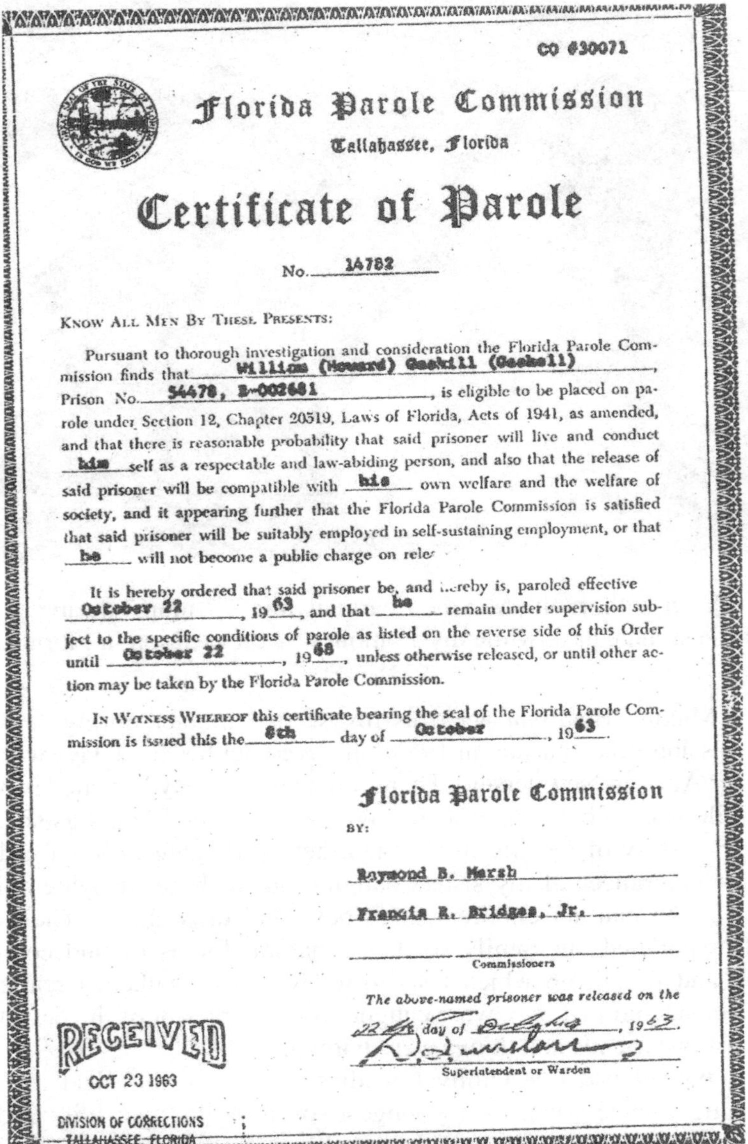

Author's Collection

224

Soon, Bill met his future spouse - we'll call her "Miss J" - through an ex-inmate buddy. "Miss J" was from a south suburb called Blue Island. After getting to know each other in and around Chicago, Bill grabbed his latest flame and took one more trip to get some kicks on Route 66. They were married on December 18, 1969 in Phoenix Arizona.

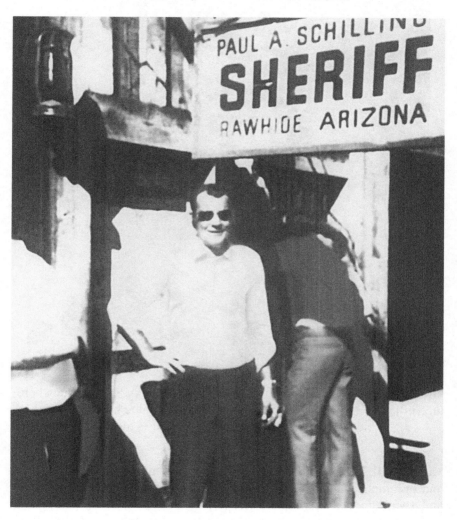

Bill visits one of his old friends to apply for a job.
He had plenty of experience with various law enforcement techniques.
"Miss J" was attracted to his 1940's style "bad boy" attitude.
Courtesy "Miss J"

The couple bought a house and settled down in the desert town. "Miss J" had significant organizational skills, which landed her a responsible management position at a Phoenix TV station. A smart kid!

225

Bill with a buddy enjoying a Budweiser and a Lucky Strike somewhere not-in-jail in 1969. Notice the right hand grasping the beer can. You can see the tip of Bill's right index finger is missing.
Courtesy "Miss J"

Bill, however, mastered a skill set that mired him in low paying and minimum wage jobs. Not much demand for a tenth grade dropout and two-time convicted felon who spent a total of 16 years in two different state penitentiaries. Add onto to that resume' a Bad Conduct Discharge from the Navy, and you have a fellow who might appear, on the surface, to be a risky employee unless you had the heart of Gandhi or were drafting your workforce from the short end of Schindler's List.

"Miss J" soon figured out that she might be better off not anchored to this fellow. After three years, she divorced Bill. Lucky for him, she remained his friend throughout the years leading up to his death. When he got violently ill in 1985, "Miss J" nurtured him back to health.

She shared her Halstead Street house with him in Phoenix. That lasted about a year and then she sent him packing. The 58 year-old Bandit moved into a local flophouse and stayed there for the remainder of his days.

His love of Budweiser beer continued throughout his 4th and 5th decades of life. He ate aspirin like candy during those years in the belief that it would minimize the pain from his hangovers. One sweltering summer day, paramedics rushed Bill to the hospital. "Miss J" went to his apartment to gather some of his personal items and was greeted with a crimson mess: bed sheets, towels and rugs spotted with dried blood as well as a pot on the floor next to his bed full to the brim. He had been spitting up blood for two weeks.

The temperature in Phoenix was 104 degrees on August 4th, 1989, when the Bandit's story ended in a cool hospital bed. Like his brother Lawrence, 62 year-old William Howard Gaskell was buried in a pauper's grave. His final resting place is in Mesa, Arizona. RIP.

Since "Miss J" kept his last name, the hospital that cared for Bill chased after her to get the cash-money for those huge medical bills. Well that didn't work. They had to eat that one.

AND SO IT GOES.....

Sometimes we dream and listen to the echoes of yesterday. This instant in time is preceded by all those now-invisible, non-re-livable moments that we call memories. A person (me) can spend hours trying to dig up those tiny fragments of life, pleasant and dreadful, just to figure out how it all fits together.

I'm sure we have all come to a point of introspective reflection and asked *"How did I get here?"* A damned good question! These incredible journeys of ours are unpredictable and seemingly randomly embellished with a mystic collage of eclectic, sedentary, dynamic, annoying and mundane creatures, characters and coauthors that unwittingly helped us compose our personal chronicle of days gone by.

Flo and Bill didn't plan their escapades in advance. I'm sure Flo and Wally married with high ideals hoping to make a happy family. Influences and circumstances forced their hands and the fates took control. They are all gone now, lost in the dust of future's rush.

OK, so maybe I'm trying to be too poetic here, struggling to find the right period on this long sentence bequeathed to me, forcing upon me the responsibility to make sense of it all for my friends, relatives and, ultimately, myself. At least this story ends with nobody getting a "cap in their ass". Oh, and Flo has one more thing to say.

Bye bye. Bye.
Author's Collection